1931                                          160

A

# A TREASURY OF
# MIDDLE ENGLISH VERSE

# A TREASURY OF
# MIDDLE ENGLISH VERSE

### SELECTED AND RENDERED
### INTO MODERN ENGLISH
### BY
### MARGOT ROBERT ADAMSON
*Author of* "A Northern Holiday," *etc.*

"Into Inglis tonge to rede
For the love of Inglis lede,
Inglis lede of merri Inglonde.

Cursor Mundi, *c.* 1260

LONDON
AND TORONTO
J. M. DENT AND SONS LTD.
NEW YORK: E. P. DUTTON & CO. Inc.

# INTRODUCTION

When George Bannatyne, in the year 1568, "in time of pest," to beguile the tedium of quarantine, compiled his own anthology, and made thereby all later students or mere lovers of our earlier literature his perpetual debtors, he apologised for his handiwork in rhyme. Bannatyne was a better copyist than poet; but his words still admirably serve all those who, in lesser degree, may follow in his tastes. I venture to modernise his "uncouth accents":

"Ye reverent readers, this work revolving right,
  If ye get crimes, correct them to your might,
  And curse no clerks that cunningly them wrote,
  But blame me boldly brought this book to light . . .
  Who late began to learn and to translate."

The following poems are "translated" or transliterated somewhat in Bannatyne's use of the word. With the utmost possible fidelity to sense, rhyme and rhythm, I have tried to render them, so that they may be read easily as poems, without a glossary or notes. At times I have rather left or given imperfect rhymes and scansion than have to alter appreciably the original. I am sadly aware that there are places where this faithfulness has led me into what the critical may feel to be too faulty grammar or uncouth constructions. I can

8087

only offer my humble apologies for these flaws in craftsmanship. It is a regrettable fact, too well known to translators, that the better a poem is the more difficult is it to make the slightest variation and not spoil. But I think I may honestly assure readers that there is no poem here differs further from the original than the copyist's variations do that strew the margins of the texts.

The student may ask indeed: Why transliterate at all? But in the prospectus of the Early English Text Society, to whose priceless volumes nine-tenths of these poems are due, there is a moving note: "The Society's experience has shown the very small number of the inheritors of the speech of Cynwulf, Chaucer and Shakspeare, who care two guineas a year for the records of that speech." Having myself long loved these poems, I hoped that by smoothing slightly the strangeness of their tongues they could be so given that they might be better known and liked by others. Their beauty and interest did not seem all to depend on old wording or strange grammar. I can only hope that readers may feel I have been successful in a labour of love. That labour could have, for me, no truer reward than that others should be moved to frequent more freely the original texts of these rhymes, by such curiosity or pleasure as I may have been fortunate enough to raise in them.

I have limited my selection to shorter lyrics, with one exception, self-contained. And I have selected those that struck most on my own interest or liking, trusting that if one reader felt so about them, others might be of the same mood. For these originals I am endebted wholly to the printed works of the scholars, having myself no knowledge of manuscripts.

The greater number of these poems have been preserved for us in manuscripts such as the Vernon MS., etc., personal anthologies collected together haphazardly by individuals now unknown. Some of these collectors, like Richard Hill or Bishop Sheppey, have left names; but they are few. Thus in almost every instance it is impossible to assign an exact date to a poem. A date in decades may be given to a whole MS., but how new or old a poem was when first copied even the most careful textual analysis finds it hard to say. The earliest given here come from "An Old English Miscellany" (E.E.T.S., No. 49), to which Richard Morris, the editor, gave the date of *circa* 1250; the latest are the lyrics from an MS. in the British Museum, reproduced by E. B. Read in "Anglia," No. 33, and dated by him temp. Henry VIII.

Few of the authors have left us their names. The earliest is William Heribert, a Franciscan friar, who died in 1333, and stumbled into beauty with the poem I have entitled "Behold thy Mother and thy Brother." Then there is John Grimstone, another Franciscan, who died in 1372; Richard de Castre who made or copied his lovely prayer about 1430, and A. Godswhen, whom Richard Wright, in his "Reliquiæ Antiquæ," dates as temp. Henry VI. Some poems belong to greater men than these. "The Ballad of Kynd Kittock" is certainly by the great William Dunbar; "Jerusalem Rejoice for Joy" and "On the Resurrection of Christ" are attributed to him, though H. B. Baildon, his editor, looks askance at them. "My Truest Treasure" is in the same case with regard to Richard Rolle. The bitter-tongued Laurence Minot jibed at the Scots somewhere between 1330 and 1360. The others have gone from us nameless. Gladly would we know more of the author of "This World Fares but as a Fantasy" and the other refrain poems of the Vernon MS.; and did the student who wrote the fragment of "The Irish Dancer" on the margin of his law text-book invent or only remember? But the wonder is rather what has survived, escaping oblivion, than the amount that has been saved. What we have we owe to a fugitive and unordered love. These lyrics are like wild flowers of yesteryear, pressed casually in some vanished spring between the leaves of time.

In transcribing I have been as faithful as is in my power, but in some instances the English tongue has so branched and changed since these poems were written that certain points still require a little elucidation. Thus some of the quality of "Earth upon Earth"—a poem with a wide provenance, of which Miss Hilda Murray has collected all the known variations in E.E.T.S., No. 141, my own version is from the rich Lambeth MS. dated *circa* 1430—is lost if it is forgotten how completely the order of Middle England, and indeed the whole medieval civilisation, was based on land and how totally wealth, honour, worldly position and prosperity were expressed in ownership of land or, as our plain-spoken poet would say, of earth by earth. Again, in this poem, in the sixth verse, the oldest in the poem, the word *shroud* has the particular sting that at the time it meant not only grave-clothes but any kind of garment. Also, the word *kind* meant not only then its usual adjectival sense or even the noun one of kind or sort, it also signified *nature*. For example, in "Piers Plowman" Dame Nature is Dame Kynd. Thus in "Mercy Passeth Everything" there is this double meaning in the line "nor is there so unkind a beast," i.e. when you are unkind you are not only that, you are also unnatural. This double significance gives a richness to the thought in

xii

verse four of "Do Mercy before thy Judgment" not directly apparent. All through the book this double value must be remembered. Sometimes it is used in its simpler modern meaning, but it is nearly always capable of the deeper use. Again, in "Do Mercy before thy Judgment," I must ask the reader, for the poem's sake, to pronounce the last word of the refrain as a trisyllable.

To bring out the full intention in "There is a Flower," I have had to double the word *solace* into "solace and pride of place," since the one word then meant both solace and supreme. "Saint John to borrow," expanded in a "Greeting on New Year's Morning," was a common form at the time of adieu, a sort of "God be wi' you," based, as our author uses it, on the legend that Saint John the Evangelist lived a hundred years. Again in "Veni Coronaberis" the line "come cleaner than crystal to my cage" loses in my version a lovely pun of the original where *cage* also signifies high-seat. In "Grey Eyes" the desire of an exact rhyme has made the lover say, in the last verse, that he would be *heard* in his lady's breast, when actually he would be *hid*. For the same reason, the Jolly Shepherd Wat refers to Saint Joseph's round *cap*, when truly it is his *cape*. These are instances which show both the exactitudes and inexactitudes of my task. On the other hand, it is in the text itself that Malkin in "A Little Sooth Sermon" is so modern as to "give the glad eye," though, in the next line, her rosary is truly not only shut up in her chest, but definedly at its very bottom.

Except for certain instances, the poems are all rendered complete. I have dared to omit from the " Land of Cockayne" the concluding particular satire on monasticism, feeling that, to-day, its crude-spoken and bitter flavour marred somewhat the earlier rhapsody on "the paradise of food and drink, forever haunting the imagination of the hungry Middle Ages," the elder Breughel has so immortalised in paint. May I also add that the paradise referred to so disparagingly therein is not Heaven, but the Garden of Eden, the Earthly Paradise, the country "west of Spain" Columbus was seeking? The curious will find the whole original in F. J. Furnivall's delightful Supplement to "The Transactions of the Philological Society" for 1858. In "Veni Coronaberis" I have omitted one verse hopelessly corrupt in the original text; and in "Mercy Passeth Everything" and "A Lamentation of the Virgin" two verses from each where I could by no manner of means preserve reason, rhyme and resemblance to the original. In both cases they were repetitive rather than expressive.

In the beautiful "O Mighty Lady" from the Hengwert MS., printed by F. J. Furnivall in "The Transactions of the Philological Society" for 1880-1, I have dared to disagree with my authority as to the limit of the poem. I have been so bold as to be well-nigh sure that two poems have been written as one, and acted accordingly, transcribing the first seven verses and omitting the latter eight. In "Since I for Love," from the Makculloch MS., I have dared to supply in the seventh verse two lost rhyme-endings. The sense of the lines made them almost a certainty.

In two instances I have permitted myself wilfully to omit. In "Farewell this World" I have left out from the great third verse two tail lines of most vile doggerel. The author who could end that verse with a jingle of gross stupidity surely deserves of any after transcriber the charity that they cut the defacing couplet away? The reader who desires the offending tag will find it in "Songs and Carols from Richard Hill's Commonplace

Book," edited by R. Dyboski (E.E.T.S., extra series, No. 101). The second case is more complicated. In "Religious, Political and Love Poems, mostly from the Lambeth MS.," edited by F. J. Furnivall (E.E.T.S., No. 15), there are, side by side, "Filius Regis Mortuus Est" from the Lambeth MS., c. 1430, and "Resurexit" from the Harleian MS., c. 1420. Both poems have the same first verse, the same refrain half-way through, the same metrical arrangement. Whether they are one poem twice written by one author or two poems on one theme by two authors, it is not in my knowledge to suggest. Here, I have dared to take all but the last two verses from "Filius Regis" and joined as second part to them the whole Harleian version, with the omission of the first three verses.

In "Pilgrims at Sea" I have left the cries of the sailors exactly as they come in the text. I do not know if the author's nautical knowledge may have been at fault. "These be high matters, my Lord." In Wright's "Reliquiæ Antiquæ" there are two very similar versions of the piece I have christened "Mirabile Dictu," one from an MS. in the Advocates' Library, one from one in the Cambridge Public Library. These I have used both in one; since that remarkable work is one the reciter might obviously vary and alter to suit his audience. My apologies are due to Signor Rat therein; for reasons of rhyme I have made him riddle when actually he played on the rebeck. And I confess to a doubt as to the culinary accuracy of my rendering of some of the recipes at that singular banquet.

I have included a group of very humble wayside flowers in the "Three Devout Fragments" from "An Old English Miscellany," and the "Pater and Credo" from the Makculloch MS. In one form or another these rhymed scraps of devotion strew all the earlier collections. Their merit may not be great, but they have about them a strange pathos of familiarity. In their simplicity they speak for so many silenced hearts!

In one of the negro Spirituals, a world closely akin in many things to the medieval, there is a line "But I'll talk about you when I get on my knees." The world of middle English did a lot of talking on its knees. Is not one of Rolle's Works entitled abruptly and characteristically "A Talking of the Love of God"? About these poems in their originals there is a strong flavour of direct speech; but, as M. Emil Male observed of the great period of Gothic art, the effigies, like these poets, have their eyes open to look God in the face. The sunset was darkening over that era when they closed them in the sombre shadows of "Farewell This World." Early England had a grisly particularity in the detail of corruption, witness the macabre Debate of the Soul and Body at Parting, but the melancholia of mortality— *timor mortis conturbat me'*—only gathers its full note at the end of their poetry. It is in signal of that end that I have included here "The Prologue" to Sir David Lyndsay's "A Satire of the Three Estates," played before the king and court at Linlithgow on Twelfth Day, 1539. Without too great hyperbole, one might say that what largely then began, both for good and for ill, was the end of the Middle Ages.

Where the manuscripts gave no titles, I have given them to the poems for convenience of identification. Thus, for example, I have followed Miss Day's note in her introduction to "The Wheatley MS." (E.E.T.S., No. 155) in calling the "Hymn to the Virgin," taken therefrom, "A Very Popular Prayer." She dates its first appearance in English *circa* 1285.

I must make one apology. As a Scot I must apologise to the verbal patriotism of the sensitive, that, without indication, I have in a collection of middle English poetry included six poems that are technically in Middle Scots.

I am, as a latter-day compiler, in debt to the whole printed world of middle English poetry, to the poets and editors I have read and not copied, and to the ones I have. I trust that both poets and editors, in this world and the next, will accept my humblest gratitude. Indeed I owe them more than I have any words to say. I would also crave leave to offer a word of my thanks to that generous stepmother of literature and learning, the London Library. It was on those crowded shelves I first learnt, not to love these poems, but to wish to make others like them. Never could I tell what coloured lyric butterfly I might not find, glowing, shut between the pages of " Learned Societies, etc."

When some six hundred years ago the author of "Cursor Mundi" set out with his wish to write—

> "Into Inglis tonge to rede
>  For the love of Inglis lede,
>  Englis lede of merri Inglond"

he committed us all. I have tried to do my best herein, and for the same reason. And, if the reader finds faults in these poems together with their beauties, I trust he or she will rightly assign the shares, the beauty to them and the faults to me.

MARGOT ROBERT ADAMSON

*July* 1929

# TEXTS AND AUTHORITIES CONSULTED

*An Old English Miscellany.* Edit. Rev. R. Morris. E.E.T.S., 49.

*The Middle English Poem "Erthe upon Erthe."* Edit. Hilda Murray. E.E.T.S., 141.

*The Minor Poems of the Vernon MS.* Edit. C. Horstmann and F. J. Furnivall. E.E.T.S., 98, 117.

*Political, Religious and Love Poems,* etc. Edit. F .J. Furnivall. E.E.T.S., 15.

*Hymns to the Virgin and Christ,* etc. Edit. F. J. Furnivall. E.E.T.S., 24.

*Religious Pieces in Prose and Verse from the Thornton MS.* Edit. C. G. Perry. E.E.T.S., 26.

*The Wheatley MS.* Edit. Mabel Day. E.E.T.S., 155.

*Songs and Carols from Richard Hill's Commonplace Book.* Edit. R. Dyboski. E.E.T.S., 101.

*Poems from the Harleian MS.* Edit. T. Wright. Percy Society.

*Specimens of Early English Carols.* Edit. T. Wright. Percy Society.

*Songs and Carols from a Fifteenth Century MS.* Edit. T. Wright. Percy Society.

*Reliquiæ Antiquæ.* Edit. T. Wright and J. C. Halliwell. 1843.

*The Bannatyne MS.* Vol. II. Edit. W. Todd Ritchie. S.T.S.

*The Makculloch MS.* Edit. G. Stevenson. S.T.S.

*Altenglische Sprachproben.* Vol. I. Edit. T. Matzer. 1863.

*Religious Lyrics of the Fourteenth Century.* Edit. Carlton Brown. 1924.

*Fourteenth Century Prose and Verse.* Edit. K. Sizam. 1921.

*The Poems of William Dunbar.* Edit. H. B. Baildon. 1907.

*The Poetical Works of Sir David Lyndsay.* Edit. D. Laing. 1871.

*Transactions of the Philological Society.* 1858.

*Transactions of the Philological Society.* 1880-1.

*Anglia*, Vol. XX, 1898.

*Anglia*, Vol. XXXIII, 1908.

*Anglia*, Vol. XLII, 1918.

*Specimens of the Early English Poets.* Edit. G. Ellis. 1803.

*Specimens of Middle English Literature.* Edit. R. Morris and W. Skeat.

# CONTENTS

xxii

# A SONG OF THE PASSION

SUMMER is come and winter gone,
The days grow long,
And the birds every one
Rejoice in song:
But strong
Care holds me bound,
For all the joy that is found
In the land:
All for a child,
That is so mild
Of His hand.


This child so mild and of dear rank
And eke great mind,
Long He me by bush and bank,
Sought to find.
He had found me
For an apple off a tree
Fast bound:
He broke the thong
That was so strong,
With His wound.

I

That child so wild and so bold
For me stooped low,
For me to Jews He was sold;
They Him did not know:
So said they "Let it be!
Nail Him upon a tree
On a hill:
But first we
Scorn over Him
Will spill."

Jesus is that child's name,
King of all lands:
Of the King they made game
Smote Him with their hands:
Smitten upon a tree,
They gave Him wounds two and three:
Lifted up
Of bitter drink
They to Him
A sore cup.

Suffered not He the rood tree,
The Life of us all,
It might not other be
But we
Were scalded all,
And boiled in hell,
Which never was sweet
Withal;
Nor might save us power
Of castle nor tower,
Nor hall.

Maid and Mother that stood,
Mary full of grace,
She wept tears all of blood,
Wailed in that place;
The trace ran of His blood;
Changed were flesh and blood
And His face.
He was ta'en
As deer are slain
In the chase.


Death He dared, that sweet Man,
High upon the rood:
He washed our sins, every one,
With His sweet blood.
With the flood He went down,
Broke the gates of that prison
That stood,
And chose thence out
Them that were
Good.


He rose on the third day
And sat on His throne:
He will come at Doom's day
To judge us, each one.
Groan he may and weep sore,
The man that dies without the law,
Alone.
Grant us, Christ,
With Thine uprising
To be gone!

Old Eng. Miscell., *c.* 1250

3

# A LITTLE SOOTH SERMON

*Or Manners and Morals seen in the Thirteenth
Century*

HARKEN all good men,
Sit ye quietly down:
And I will tell you
A little sooth sermon.
Well wot ye all,
Though I do not it tell,
How Adam our forefather
A-down fell to hell.
Shamelessly lost he
The bliss that he had,
By greed and by pride
When no need he had.
He took the apple off the tree
To him was forbidden:
So rueful a deed
Never was done:
He made himself to hell fall,
And after him his children all:
There he was until the hour
Our Lord thence brought him with His power;
He freed them with His very blood,
That He shed upon the rood.

4

To death He gave Himself for all,
Though we were so keen to fall.
All backbiters
They make hell's way:
Robbers and reivers
Them that man-slay:
Lechers and lusters
Thither shall wend:
There shall their joy
Have a hard end.
All those false dealers
The fiend will meet:
Brewers and bakers,
For all men they cheat.
They lower the gallon
And fill it spice:
Other men's silver
To their purse to entice.
Both they make feeble
Their bread and their ale;
But to get silver
They'll tell any tale.
Good men for God's love
Leave such sin:
For at the end it faileth
Heaven to win!
All priests' wives
I wot shall be forlorn:
Those parsons I guess
Shall be overborne.
And those proud young men
That go after Malkin,
And those proud maidens
That run after Jankin:

At church and to market,
When they come by,
They run all together
And talk light love and sly.
When they to church come
On a holy day
They spy round the other
To see if they may.
She beholdeth Watkin
With a glad eye,
At home is her paternoster,
In her chest left by.
Of masses and matins
Mind keeps she nought,
Wilkin and Watkin
Are all her thought.
Robin will Gilot
Take to have ale:
Sit there together
And tell her a tale.
He will pay for her drink
And see to his game,
At eve to go with him,
She thinketh no shame.
Her sire and her dame
Threaten her to beat:
She'll not forgo Robin
For any threat.
But he'll make excuses,
Come no more her nigh
When her body showeth
Childing is nigh.
Good men for God's love
Forsake your sins,

At the end they fail you
Heaven to win!
Pray we Saint Mary,
For her gentle mood,
By the tears that she wept,
For her Son's blood:
Even as He God is
For her interceding
He may to bliss of heaven
All of us bring!
                    Amen.

              Old Eng. Miscell., *c.* 1250

LET true love amongst us be
Without an ending!
And Christ our blessing be,
Give us His tending,
Give us that we may flee
From all defiling,
From the fiend and his foul glee,
All his beguiling.

Hold we worthy that Lord God
That hither us brought:
He had with us the mildest mood
When He us wrought;
And after, hanged upon the rood,
Our help He sought,
With His flesh and with His blood,
Us all He bought.

Blessed be such an atheling,
Pity us He would.
He is our best king
We should by Him hold.
And we are all His offspring,
Know it we should,
For He shaped us and each thing
Of the earth's mould.

Christ hath us of earth wrought,
To earth He will us send:
By His death we were all bought
From the fiend's bend:

He hath it all bethought,
The beginning and the end,
How that we are hither brought,
And whither we shall wend.

If we be righteous
And love our Knight,
And do His service
With all our might:
Then need we never fear,
By day nor night.
We shall in paradise
Shine very bright.

This world is nigh an end,
Death nigheth near:
Hence we shall all wend,
We may not stay here.
The Doom is nigh at hand!
If we let shrift go bye,
Christ will us from Him send
Because of that lie.

Let us hold by each word
That Christ will us teach,
He is our life and our death's Food,
He is our Leach.
Be we with others mild of mood
In work and speech;
Else will our Lord God's
Doom to us reach.

With good prayer and good thought
We should to Christ cry,
To give us pity of our wrong,
For our foolery,

For our sins that be so strong,
For each evil deed,
When He cometh us among
He will us with Him lead!

Our Lord Christ will lead us,
The Heaven-guide this:
If we will evil flee
We need not it miss.
Well to him that shall there be
He may have peace:
He may ever Christ see,
With joy enough and bliss.

There is day without night,
The half has no man heard,
There full peace without fight:
Well is God honoured.
There truth is seen aright
By all alike,
Rich man and poor man equal,
Churl even with knight.

True love lives them among,
Pity and righteousness,
Right belief and true tongue,
Friendship and gentleness:
Dwells there no fraud or wrong,
No wrath nor idleness,
There is joy and merry song,
Without fickleness.

If we would thither go
To that rich dwelling,

Idleness and sloth our foe
And wrath and hating:
Pride and malice, the fiend's gin,
Before our end,
We must forsake and every sin,
And make amend.

We should have amongst us aye
Sooth love and kinship,
Working what Christ doth say,
Earnest in fellowship;
We should love all the way,
We are all kinsmen;
And pray both night and day
While we are live men.

Sooth love is good and mild,
Is no wise stern;
It is neither proud nor wild,
Nor doth coveting yearn.
That folk that are with wrath defiled
And will not to Him turn,
Jesus, that is sweet Mary's child,
Will from his riches spurn.

The sooth love is righteous
Nor hath a hungry hand;
Amid the folk that are righteous
He will aye stand.
Our Lord Christ that almighty is
Loose us of his band,
And lead us into heaven's bliss,
Set us at His right hand!

Old Eng. Miscell., c. 1250

# THREE SORRY THINGS

EACH day come to me tidings three
And sore and sorry things they be:
The first from hence that I shall go,
The other when I do not know.
The third it is my greatest care:
I know not whither I shall fare.

Old Eng. Miscell., *c.* 1250

# FORTUNE

WEAL, thou art a crooked thing, uneven in thy
    serving!
Thou treatest a wretch well enough but not through
    his deserving.
With wealthy men thou keepst good faith, in bliss to
    make them sure:
Even to speak unto the rich thou givest not to the poor!

Old Eng. Miscell., c. 1250

## SALVE REGINA!

BLESSED be thou, Lady,
     Full of heaven's bliss,
Sweet flower of Paradise,
     Mother of mildness!
Pray thou Jesu Christ thy Son
     That He may lead me,
That in the land whereso I be
     He may not need me.


Of thee fair Lady, mine orison
     I will begin!
Thy dear sweet Son's love
     Teach me to win.
Well oft I sigh and sorrow make
     Nor may quit therein,
But thou through thy mild mood
     Bring me out of sin!


Often I seek mercy,
     Thy sweet name I call:
My flesh is foul, the world is false,
     Look Thou I do not fall.

Lady free, shield thou me
　　　From the pain of hell,
And send me in unto that bliss
　　　No tongue may tell.


Mine works, Lady,
　　　They make me wan:
Very oft I cry and call,
　　　Hear thou me for them!
But I gain thy help of thee
　　　None other can:
Help thou me, full well thou may'st,
　　　Thou helpest many a man!


Blessed be thou, Lady,
　　　So fair and so bright;
All mine hope is upon thee
　　　By day and by night.
Help, through thy most gentle mood
　　　For good well thou might,
That I never for men's sake
　　　Forgo thy light.


Bright and sheen, Queen of Heaven,
　　　I beg thy Son hear:
The sins that I have done
　　　They grieve me sore.
Very oft thee have I forsaken,
　　　I will do it nevermore,
Lady, for thy sake
　　　Make truth of foe's war.

Blessed be thou, Lady,
    So fair and friendly,
Pray thou Jesu Christ thy Son
    That He so send me
Whatsoever land where I may be,
    When I hence wend,
That I may in paradise
    Dwell without end.


Bright and sheen, starry Queen,
    So light me and clear
In this false fickle world
    So lead me and steer
That I at mine ending day
    May have no fiend to fear:
Jesu, with Thy sweetest blood
    Thou boughtst me very dear!


Jesu, Saint Mary's Son,
    Hear Thou Thy mother kind:
Of Thee I dare ask nought,
    To her I make my mind.
Thou do that for her sake,
    So clean make me,
That I at day of doom
    Fear not to look on Thee!

Egerton MS., c. 1250

# HOW HOLY CHURCH IS UNDERFOOT

AWHILE back St. Peter was calléd Simon.
  So quoth Our Lord to him, "Thou shalt be
    called stone,
I will mine holy church set thee upon."
They that should be wise for her, her foes are grown:
Of all her former friends, now stayeth by her none!
Once there was Simon, now there is simony,
That greater part hath ruined of the clergy.
Pray we to Our Lord Christ that He her saving be
For His sweet Mother's love, the Saint Mary.
After that Saint Peter was pope in Rome,
That is the head, and ought to be, of Christendom;
Clement and Gregory that after him come
They had grief and sorrows oft times and some,
For they held Christ's men by love and mild mood
And eke Holy Church withouten servitude.
So she stood full fast and a time held her ground:
Now men cast about with mark and with pound,
With silver and with gold to bring her to the ground.
Nor is there any man for her will suffer death or wound!
Saint Thomas suffered for her, a death unright,
The Archbishop Stephen for her did fight,
And Saint Edmund after, full truthfully him dight,
To hold her in worship, he did all his might.
But now is Holy Church under an evil hand:

All worry at her that dwell in the land.
Bishops and clerks, knights and villager,
Kings and earls breathe hatred at her:
And the Pope himself who should be her hold
He has the takings of silver and gold,
Marks and pounds with right and with wrong,
He lets them do their work that are over-strong!
Alas for her in this our day she is so under men's feet!
Pray we all to Jesus Christ He with help her may meet,
For His sweet Mother's love that is so true and sweet,
Pray we in this our life we may soon see it!

Amen.

Old Eng. Miscell., *c.* 1250

# NOW SPRINGS THE SPRAY

NOW springs the spray:
   All for Love I am so sick
Sleep not I may!

As I rode this latter day
For my playing,
Saw I where a little may
Began to sing:
" Cold clay to him cling!
Woe is he in love-longing
Shall live alway."

Soon as I heard that merry note,
Thither I drew,
I found her in an arbour sweet
Under a bough,
With joy enow:
Soon I asked, " Thou merry may,
How singest thou
This way?"

Then answerèd that maiden sweet
With words few:
" My leman did me greet,

Promised love true.
He has changed anew,
If I may
It shall him rue
This very day."

Now springs the spray:
All for love I am so sick
Sleep not I may!

Lincoln's Inn MS., *c.* 1300

# THE LAND OF COCKAYNE

FAR in the sea and west of Spain,
  There is a country called Cockayne;
There is no land 'neath Heaven's bliss
As good, as fair as that land is.
Though paradise be merry and bright,
Cockayne it is a fairer sight.
For what in paradise is seen
But grass and flowers and branches green?
Though there is joy from a glad root,
There there is no meat but fruit;
There is no hall, nor bower, nor bench,
But water a man's thirst to quench.
There there are but two men to go,
Eli and Enoch also.
They may sorry go and sore,
Where there are of folk no more!
In Cockayne is meat and drink,
Without care, nor stress, nor swink.
The meat is spiced, the drink is clear,
No raisin-wine or dull slops there!
I say for sooth and no doubt bear,
There is no land on earth its peer:
There is 'neath Heaven no land I wis
Of so mickle joy and bliss.
There is many a sweet sight,

All is day, there is no night;
There is no wrangling, nor no strife,
There is no death but always life;
There is no lack of meat or cloth,
There is no man nor woman wrath;
There is no serpent, wolf or fox,
There no charger and no ox;
There no sheep, nor swine nor goat,
There is no squire, God it wot!
There no breeding and no studs;
That land is full of other goods!
There is nor fly, nor flea, nor louse,
In clothes, in town, in bed, nor house;
There is no thunder, sleet, or hail,
Nor no vile worm, nor any snail;
Nor no storm or rain or wind:
There is no man nor woman blind:
But all is game and joy and glee,
Well for him that there may be!
There are rivers great and fine
Of oil and milk, of honey and wine.
Water serveth there no thing,
But for the sight or else washing.
There is every manner of fruit
And all is solace and joy's root.
There there is a fair abbèy,
Of white monks and also grey;
There there be bowers and halls,
And all of pastries are the walls,
Of flesh, of fishes, of rich meat,
The most delicious man may eat.
Flour cakes are the shingles all
Of church and cloister, bower and hall.
The pinnacles are fat puddings,

Rich meats of princes and of kings;
Man thereof may eat his fill,
All is right and nought comes ill;
All is common, for young and old,
For stout and lean, for meek and bold.
There is a cloister fair and light,
Broad and long, a seemly sight.
The pillars of that cloister all
Are fine turnèd of crystal,
With their base and capital
Of green jasper and red coral.
In the meadow is a tree,
Sooth, a delight it is to see!
The root is ginger and galingale,
The shoots are candied ginger pale,
Choice maces are the flower,
The rind cinnamon of sweet savour,
The fruit gillyflowers of good smack.
Of cucumbers there is no lack;
There are roses red of hue,
And lilies beautiful to view;
There they wither nor day nor night,
But blow for ever sweet to sight.
There are three wells in that abbey,
Of treacle and of balsam they,
Of balm and mulled wine spiced and good,
Ever running, aye in flood.
Of these fountains all the mould,
Precious jewels and red gold;
There are pearls and sapphires there,
Carbuncles and crystals fair,
Smaragdus, hyacinth, chrysophras,
Beryl, onyx, and topaz,
Amethyst and chrysolite,

Chalcedony and epatite.
There are birds many and all,
Throstle, thrush and nightingale,
Laverocks and the woodwale,
And other birds beyond my tale,
That stint never of their might,
Merrily singing day and night.
Yet would I have you more to wit:
The geese a-roasted on the spit,
Fly to that abbey—God it wot!—
And cackle " Geese all hot! All hot!"
They bring there garlic in plenty,
The best dressed that man may see;
And the larks, in good troth,
Light adown in a man's mouth,
Trussed and toasted and baked well,
Powdered with cloves and cinnamel.
There is no asking you to drink,
There enow at once you drink!

\*       \*       \*       \*       \*

There is no land 'neath heaven's bliss,
So fair, so good as that land is!

Bodl. MS., 13th cent.

# AUTUMN

NOW wither rose and lily flower,
  That awhile bare that sweet savour
In summer, that sweet tide;
Nor is queen so sure, upright,
Nor lady in her bower so bright
Death shall not by her glide.
Whoso will fleshly lust forgo
And heaven's bliss abide
On Jesu be his thinking so,
Was wounded in His side.

From Peterborough on a morning,
As I was wending for my pleasing,
On my folly I methought;
Weeping, I sent my mourning
To her that bore the heaven's King,
For mercy her besought.
Lady, pray thy Son for us
That hath us dearly bought,
And shield us from the loathly house
That the fiend hath wrought.

Mine heart for my deeds had dread,
For sins wherewith my flesh I fed

D

And followed all my time,
That I wist not whither I should be led
When I lay on my death's bed,
To joy or else to pine.
In a lady mine hope is,
Mother and virgin;
We shall go into heaven's bliss
Through her medicine.


Better is her medicine
Than any mead or any wine—
Her herb smelleth sweet—
Out of Caithness into Dublin
Is there never a leach so fine
Our sorrows to meet.
Man that feeleth any sore
And will his follies quit,
Without gold or treasure more
He may be sound and sweet.


Of penance is this plaster all,
And ever serve her I shall
Now and all my days alive;
Now is he free was erst in thrawl
All through that lady, gentle and small—
Praised be her joys five!
Whereso any sick is
Hither hie blythe,
Through her be brought to bliss,
Both maiden and wife.

For He that died in His body on the tree
On our sins have pity,
That welded heaven's bowers!
Woman with thy gaiety,
Though thou art so white and bright to see
Think upon God's showers;
Fall shall all the flowers.
Jesu have mercy upon us
That all the world honours!

Harl. MS., c. 1310

# BY LONGING I AM LED

BY longing I am led,
　　On earth I am grown mad,
A maiden marreth me;
I grieve, I groan unglad,
Seldom I see her, sad,
That seemly is to see:
Lady, thou painest me,
To ruth thou hast me led.
Be help who sickness made;
My life longs for thee.

Lady, for all the land,
Loose me from out thy bond!
Brought I am in woe,
Have resting of thine hand,
And a kind message send
Soon, ere thou slay me so;
Restless 'mid men I go;
Men envy me and wonder;
To love it is no wonder,
I cannot let it go!

Lady, with all my might
My love on thee doth light

To praise thee while I may;
Pity and read me right,
To death thou hast me dight;
I die long ere my day;
Thou leadest all my lay.
Troth unto thee I plight
To do that I have might
While my life lasteth may.


Lilywhite her hue is,
As a rose so her red is,
That reives from me my rest.
Woman aware and wise,
Proudly she bears the prize;
Maid of the best;
This woman dwelleth in the west,
Brightest of all that is,
All heaven I hold is his
That one night were her guest!

Harl. MS., c. 1310

# SPRING

WHEN the nightingale singeth the woods waxen
       green,
Leaf and grass and blossom spring in April, I ween,
And Love is in unto mine heart with spear so keen,
Night and day my blood it drinks, my heart doth me
       teen.

I have loved all this year, and I cannot love more;
I have sighed many sighs, my dear one, thee for;
My love nighs never the nearer me and hurts me sore;
Sweet leman, think on me, I have loved thee of yore.

Sweet leman, I pray thee of love one speech,
While I live in the world so wide none other will I
       seek;
With thy love, my sweet life, my bliss thou mightst
       teach,
A sweet kiss of thy mouth might be my leech!

Sweet leman, I pray thee for a love-boon;
If thou lovest me, as men say, leman, as I ween,
And if thou wilt it be so, then look that it be seen;
So much I think upon thee, my face waxes all green.

Between Lincoln and Land's End, Northampton and
       London,
Wot I of none so fair a may as her to whom I am
       bound!
Sweet leman, I pray thee love me a little time;
I will weep my song on her that I long for and make
       my rhyme.

Harl. MS., c. 1310

# PRISON SONGS

## I

THERE is no land has sorrow for me;
  There is no man takes heed of me:
Careful and full of grief I sigh:
Gentles, I suffer here much shame,
Help, God, for Thy sweet name,
King of Heaven high!

## II

Jesu Christ, sooth God, sooth man,
Lord, rue Thou for me:
From prison where I am
Bring me out and make me free:
I and my fellows here,
God wots that I lie not,
For other men's misdeeds
Here in this prison brought!

## III

Almighty, Well of Light,
  Of bale the help and hope,
Heaven's King, of this dwelling
  That Thou would bring us out!

Forgive them, the wicked men,
  God, if it is Thy will,
For whose guilt we be spilt
  In this prison ill!

## IV

No hope has man to live
Here that he may believe,
How so high he may ascend
Doom fells him to the ground.
Nay, had man wealth and bliss
The swifter he shall miss:
World's weal, well now I wis,
Lasts but a little sound!

## V

Maiden that bore the heaven's King,
Beseech thy Son, that sweet thing,
That He of us have rueing
And bring us from this dwelling:
For His great mildness,
Bring us from out this woe,
And His Will work it so,
In this world whereso we go,
That we may live ever and o,
Having His kindness.

                  Liber de Antiquis Legibus, 13th cent.

# THREE DEVOUT FRAGMENTS

## I

IN my defence, God me defend;
And in my doings God me fend:
When I am sick and like to die,
The Son of God have mercy on me!

Makculloch MS.

## II

### AVE

Mary full of grace, well may thou be,
God of heaven He is with thee;
Over all women blessèd may thou be,
So be the bairn that is born of thee!

## III

### IN MANUS TUAS

Love-Lord God, in hands of Thine
I bequeath this soul of mine;
Thou boughtest me with Thy death,
Love-Lord God of soothfastness!

Arundel MS., 13th cent.

33

## GREY EYES

A VEIL white as whale's bone,
  A gown of gold that goodly shone,
A kirtle that mine heart is on,
In a stead true;
Her gladness it is never gone,
While I must rue.


When she is glad
Of all the world no more I bide
Than be with her mine own, beside,
Without strife;
The care that I am in be-tied,
To wit, a wife.


Than her there is none so fairly wrought,
When she is blithely to her bed brought,
Well were he that wist her thought
And thrives there through.
Well I wot she thinks of me not;
Mine heart is woe.


How shall that one gladly sing
That thus is marrèd by mourning?

She will me to death bring,
Long ere my day.
Greet her well, that sweet thing,
With eyes grey.


Her eyes have wounded me I wis;
Her brows' bend that bringeth bliss,
Her comely mouth who that might kiss
In much mirth were.
I would change mine for his,
That is her dear!


Would her dear be so free,
And worth were it so might be,
For his one I would give three
Without trick:
From hell to heaven or sun to sea
Is none so quick,
Nor half so free.
Whoso will of love be true
Does like to me.


Hearken me, I do you tell,
In such wondrous woe I dwell,
There is no fire so hot in Hell
As for a man
That loveth dear and dare not tell
Whom it is on.

I wish her well and she me woe;
I am her friend and she my foe;
Methinketh my heart will break in two,
For sorrow and spite!
In God's greeting may she go
That veil white.


I would I were a thistlecock,
A bunting or a laverock,
Sweet bird!
Between her kirtle and her smock
I would be heard!

Harl. MS., *c.* 1310

# A SONG OF THE FIVE JOYS

HAIL to thee, Mary, maiden bright!
Teach thou me thy ways aright;
I am a sorrowful, dreary wight
As thou mayst see:
Where I in the hard pains of hell may be.


My sinful soul sigheth sore;
Lived have I in sin and care therefore.
Leave it I will and do no more.
My lady free,
Soul and body, life and death, I give to thee!


There thou layest in thy bright bower,
Lady, white as lily-flower,
An angel came from heaven's tower,
Saint Gabriel,
And said, "Lady, full of bliss, all work thee well."


Still thou stoodest and stayed naught,
Thou saidst to him the message brought,
"All His will it shall be wrought
In His ancele,"
Lady, unto thy sweet Son make us all leal!

The other joy I wot it was
As the sun that shines through glass;
So, art thou, lady, stainless
And ever shall be.
Lady, for that sweet joy, have pity on me!


The third joy, I understand;
Three kings came out of their own land
To fall before thy sweet Son's hand,
And gave Him gifts,
Myrrh, incense and gold red, as it was right.


The king was rich, the gold was red,
The incense fell to His Godhead,
Myrrh to the man that shall be dead
For our sake.
Lady, thy sweet Son at one with us make!


The fourth, it is all through His grace
When He from death to life did rise,
When that so hard He hangèd was
On the rood tree.
Lady, of all our sins make thou us free!


The fifth, thou wast to heaven brought,
The Jews thee sought and found thee not;
All thy sweet Son had wrought,
Almighty King.
Lady Mary, be our help at our ending!

Lady, for thy joys five,
Make known thy might and help us rife.
Lady Mary, Mother of Life,
With flower and fruit,
Rose and Lily thou spreadest wide, help thou our suit!


Lady Mary, well thou knowest
The fiend assails me ever fast,
Well I hope I may him off-cast
Through might of thee;
When I name thy sweetest name, I make him flee.


Thy joys are said as I can say,
My care, my sorrow I cast away,
Now help me, Lady, well as thou may,
And be my hope;
From the hard pain of hell hold thou me up.


All they that sing this song
And that lie in pains strong,
Thou lead them right where they go wrong
And have mercy
On all that trust that God was born of thee, thou fair
Lady!

               "Cursor Mundi" MS., before 1350

## "BEHOLD THY MOTHER AND THY BROTHER"

THOU woman without peer,
   Didst thine own father bear.
Great wonder 'twas
That one woman was mother
To father and her brother—
So never other was.


Thou my sister and mother—
And thy son my brother—
Who should then dread?
Who has the king for brother
And eke the queen for mother,
Well should be sped.


Dame, sister and mother,
Say to thy son, my brother,
That is doom's man,
For that thou didst him bear
To me be debonair—
My robe he hath on.

In sooth he my coat took;
Also, I find in the book
He is to me bound;
And help he will, I wot:
For love the charter wrote—
The inkhorn his wound.

I take for witnessing
The spear and the crowning,
The nails, the rood,
That he that is so kind
This ever have in mind,
That bought us with his blood.


When thou gavest him my weed,
Dame, help me thou at need,
I wot thou mayst full well,
That for no wretched guilt
I be to hell's-ward spilt—
To thee I make appeal.


Now, Dame, I thee beseech
At that day of wrath's reach,
Be by thy son's throne;
When then sins shall be sought
In word, in deed, in thought,
And speak for me one.


When I must needs appear
For my guilt here,
Before the doom's man,

E

Sister, be thou my peer,
And make him debonair
That my robe haveth on.


For I have thee and him,
That marks bearest on him
Where charity him took—
The wounds all bloody
The tokens of mercy
As teachest the holy book—
Therefore, I nothing dread,
Satan he shall nought speed
With clutches nor with crook!

Friar William Heribert, *d.* 1333

## "SCOTS WHA' HAE!" REVERSED

*For the Battle of Halidon Hill*

NOW for to tell you will I turn
Of the Battle of Bannockburn!

Scots out of Berwick and of Aberdeen
At Bannockburn ye were over-keen!
There slew ye many sackless, as it was seen,
And now has King Edward reversed it, I ween.
You are hit back again, well worth your while!
Wary with the Scots, for they are full of guile!

Where are ye Scots out of St. John's town?
The boast of your banner is all beaten down.
When ye boasting will bide, Sir Edward goes down
To kindle your care and crack your crown.
He has cracked your crown, well worth the while!
Shame betide the Scots, for they are full of guile!

Scots of Stirling were stirring and stout,
Of God nor good man had they no doubt:
Now have they, the prickers, been pricked about;
But at last Sir Edward riddled their rout.
He has routed their rout, well worth the while!
But ever have they in them but trickings and guile.

Rough-footed brogue-feet now kindles your care!
Bag-bearing boasters, your building is bare:
False wretches and forsworn, whither wilt fare?
Busk ye to Bruges, you, and bide ye there!
There, wretch, shall you dwell and weary the while:
Your dwelling in Dundee is done down for your guile!


The Scot goes to Bruges and beats about the streets;
For these English men harm he heats.
Fast makes he moan to any man he meets:
But fool friends he finds that his bale greets.
Fools deal with his talk, well worth the while!
They use in threatening but tricks and guile.


But many man threatens and speaks full ill
That sometime were better to stand—still.
The Scot in his words has much wind to spill,
But at the last Edward shall have his will.
He had his will at Berwick, well worth the while!
Scots brought him the keys—got that pay for their guile.

Lawrence Minot Colton MS., *c.* 1333

44

## FIVE JOYS

AS I rode this latter day,
By green woods to seek a play,
All my heart's thought was on a may,
The sweetest thing.
Listen, I tell you as I may
Of that sweet thing.

This maiden, sweet and free of blood,
Bright and fair, of a mild mood,
To us all she has done all good
Through her beseeching;
Of her he took both flesh and blood,
Jesus, Heaven's king.

With all my life I love that may,
She is my solace night and day;
My joy and eke my best play
And eke my love-longing;
All the better to me the day
I of her sing.

Of all things I love her most,
My day's bliss, my night's rest;
She counselleth and helpeth best

Both old and young;
Now will I tell her as I may
Five joys among.


The first joy of that woman;
When Gabriel from heaven came
And said God shall become a man
Of her be born,
And bring up out of Hell's pain
Mankind forlorn.


That other joy of that may
Was upon Christmas Day,
When Christ was born in the due way
And brought us lightness;
The star was seen before the day—
The herds bear witness.


The third joy of that lady,
That men call Epiphany,
When the kings came a weary way
To present her son,
With myrrh and gold and incense play,
That was man become.


The fourth joy we tell amain;
On Easter morrow when dawn came
Her son that had been slain
Arose with flesh and bone—
More joy than that may's then can have
Wife nor maid, none.

The fifth joy of that woman,
When her body to heaven came,
The soul unto the body, name
As it was wont to be.
Christ grant us all with that woman
That joy to see!

Pray we all to our Lady
And to the saints that dwell her by
That she of us will have mercy,
We may not miss,
In this world to have been holy
And win Heaven's bliss.

Harl. MS., c. 1310

## CONQUERING AND TO CONQUER

I SAW him with flesh all bespread; he came from the
    East.
I saw him with blood all spatterèd; he came from the
    West.
I saw that many he with him brought; he came from
    the South.
I saw that of him the world recked naught; he came
    from the North.

I come from the wedlock as a sweet spouse, that have
    my wife with me, named in one.
I come from fight, a stalwart knight that mine foe hath
    overcome.
I come from the market as a rich merchant that man-
    kind hath bought.
I come from an uncouth land as a simple pilgrim, so far
    have I sought!

He rode upon a white horse thus
That he came, man, for thee.
He rode on a red horse thus
That he was nailed on the rood tree.
He rode on a black horse thus
That he the devil overcame.
He rode on a dun horse thus
That the cloud o'er him came.

He rode on a white horse and had a bow in his hand
In token he was skilful.
He that rode on a red horse had a sword in his hand
In token he was powerful.
He that rode on the black horse had a scales in his
    hand
In token his was the right.
He that rode on the dun horse had many folk him
    following
In token his was the might.

Merton College MS., before 1366

# LOVE'S ADVENTURE

M Y love is fallen upon a may,
For love of her I fight this day.
Love's adventure no man forsaketh,
It woundeth sore when him it taketh;
Love's venture may have no rest,
Where thought is risen, there love is fast;
Love's adventure with woe is bought,
There love is true, it flitteth nought.

MS., Advocate's Lib., *c.* 1372

# MATER DOLOROSA

WHY have ye no ruth of my dear child?
　　Have ruth on me so full of mourning,
Take down from the rood my dear-worthy child
Or prick me on one rood with my darling.

More pain to me may not be done
Than to let me live in sorrow and shame;
As love me bindeth fast to my son
So let us both die, both the same.

J. Grimstone, d. 1372

# LOVE ON THE CROSS

LOVE me brought,
And Love me wrought
Man to be thy peer.
Love me fed,
And Love me led
And Love left me here.

Love me slew
And Love me drew
And Love me laid on bier.
Love is my peace;
For Love I chose
Man to buy dear.

Dread thou nought,
I have thee sought
Both by day and night!
To have thee,
Well is with me;
I have thee won in fight.

J. Grimstone, *d.* 1372

## A VERY POPULAR PRAYER

MARY Mother, well with thee!
Mary Maiden, think on me!
Mother and maid was never none,
Together, Lady, but thou alone.
Mary mother, maiden clear,
Shield me to-day from sorrow and fear.
Mary, out of sin help thou me;
And out of debt, for charity.
Mary for thy joys five,
Help me to live a clean life!
For the tears thou wept beneath the Rood,
Send me grace of daily food,
Wherewith I may me clothe and feed,
And in truth my life lead.

Help me, Lady, and all mine,
And shield us all from hell a-pine;
Shield us all from worldly shame,
And from all wicked fame:
Shield us from all villainy
And from all wicked company!
Sweet Lady, maiden mild,
Against the fiend, thou me shield.
The fiend 'gainst me would never dare,

Sweet Lady, if thou with me were!
Both by day and by night,
Dear Lady, fair and bright!

For my friends I beg thee,
That they might amended be,
Both in soul and all alive,
Mary, for thy joys five.
For my foemen I beg too,
That I and they so may do
In wrath may die nor I nor they,
Sweet Lady, I thee pray!
And they that are in good alive,
Mary, for thy joys five,
Sweet Lady, therein them hold,
Be they young or be they old:
And they that are in deadly sin,
Let them never die therein.
Sweet Lady, give them thy rede,
That they amend of their misdeed;
Mary, for thy joys all,
Let them never in sin fall!

Pray thy Son, Heaven's King,
Send me shrift, housel, and good ending!
Send me, Lady, such a grace
In Heaven's bliss to have a place.
Mary, as trust I now to thee,
These prayers grant thou to me;
And help me that I have that bliss
That never more shall fail or miss!

Amen.

Wheatley MS., c. 1290

# HOLLY AND IVY

HOLLY and Ivy made a great parley
Who should have mastery
    In lands where they go.
Then said Holly: I am free and jolly,
I will have the mastery
    In lands where we go.
Then spake Ivy: I am loud and proud
And I will have the mastery
    In lands where we go.
Then spake Holly and set him down on his knee:
I pray thee, gentle Ivy,
Do me no villainy
    In lands where we go!

                          15th cent.

# THE IRISH DANCER

I COME from Ireland,
  From the holy land
Of Ireland:
Good sir, I pray to thee,
For of Saint Charity,
Come out and dance with me
In Ireland!

Bodleian MS., 14th cent.

## MY TRUEST TREASURE

MY Truest Treasure so traitorly taken,
  So bitterly bounden with biting bands,
How soon of thy servants wast thou forsaken
And loathly for my life hurled with their hands!

My Well of my Weal so wrongly accusèd,
So pulled out of prison to Pilate at Prime;
Their wounds and their dints thou drearily dreèd
When they shot in thy sight both slaver and slime.

My Hope of my Health so hurried to hanging,
So charged with thy cross and crownèd with thorn,
So sore to thy heart thy steps they were stinging—
Methinks thy back must break; it bends overborne.

My Salve of my Sore so sorry in sight,
So naked and nailed, they rig thee on the rood,
Full helplessly hanging and heaved on a height,
They let thee stab on the stone that socketing stood.

My dear-worthy Darling, so dolefully dight,
So straightly uprighted, strained on the rood;
For thy mickle meekness, thy mercy, thy might,
Thou healed all my woes with the boon of thy blood!

My 'Fender of my Foes, so fallen on the field,
So lovingly lighting at evensong tide;
Thy mother and thy menic unlacèd thy shield—
All wept that were there, thy wounds were so wide.

My peerless Prince, as poor I thee pray,
The mind of this mirror, thou, let me not miss;
But wind up my will to be one with thee aye,
Be buried in my breast, and bring me to bliss!

R. Rolle(?) Camb. Univ. MS., 14th cent.

# STEADFAST CROSS!

STEADFAST cross, among all others,
Thou art a tree of mickle prize,
In branch and flowering such an other
I know not of in wood or rise!
Sweet the nails three
And sweet is the tree,
And sweetest is the burden that hangeth upon thee!

Merton Coll. MS., 14th cent.

# EASTER

THIS is the time Man hath o'ercome
   The fiend, robbed hell.
Look now from his service
Far you do not dwell!
Man is now made knight
And ruler o'er each thing;
Look on no earthly thing
Ye set thine ending!
For now is earthly man become
God's own brother;
Look man, in no wise
Ye change for another.

Harl. MS., c. 1370

# CHRIST ON THE CROSS

HE that seeth on the rood
    Jesus, his leman:
And how His Mother by him stood,
Sorely weeping, and Saint John:
And His side piercèd sore,
For love of thee, man:
Well should he his sins forsake,
With tears, and from them break,—
He that love can!

Harl. MS., c. 1380

# MERCY

IF never sin were, Mercy were none:
When Mercy is called, he cometh anon.

Mercy is readiest where sin is most:
Mercy is latest where sin is least.

Mercy abides and looks all day,
When men from sin will turn away.

Harl. MS., c. 1380

# MERCY PASSETH ALL THINGS

WESTWARD, under a wild wood side,
  In a wild land, there I lent.
Proud deer across the ground did glide
And lions ramping o'er the bent;
Bears, wolves, with mouths set wide,
The small beasts they tore and rent;
There, hawks unto their prey they hied;
Thereunto I made attent.
A merlin on a bird had seized,
Between his feet he it did bring;
It could not speak but thus it sighed;
"Mercy surpasseth everything."

Mercy was in that small bird's mind,
But thereof the hawk knew none;
For 'twixt his claws he did it bind
And held it still as any stone.
He did in the fashion of his kind;
Into a tree he flew anon;
There could the bird some mercy find
For on the morrow the hawk was gone.
Full still I stood myself alone
To harken how that bird 'gan sing:
"Away will wend both mirth and moan,
Mercy surpasseth everything."

How Mercy passeth strength and right,
In many manners see we may.
God ordained Mercy, most of might,
To be above his works for aye.
When dear Jesus shall be dight
To doom us upon Judgment Day,
Our sins will be so much in sight
We shall not wit what we should say;
Full fiercely Right will us assay
And blame us for our misliving;
Then dare none for us to pray
But Mercy that passeth everything.

Right would slay us for our sin,
Might would do execution;
And Righteous God will then begin
For to rehearse us His reason:
"I made thee, Man, as thou wilt mind
Of feature like to mine own fashion,
And after crept I into thy kin
And for thee I suffered passion.
Of keen thorns was the crown
Full sharp upon mine head standing,
Mine heart's blood from me ran down,
And I forgave thee everything!

" Mine heart's blood for thee 'gan bleed
To buy thee from the fiends at stake;
And I forgave thee thy misdeed.
What hast thou suffered for my sake?
I hungered, thou wouldst not me feed,
Nor never mine thirst wouldst thou slake;
When I of harbourage had great need,

Thou wouldst not me to thine house take;
But sawest me among toads black
Full long in a hard prison living.
Let see, what answer canst thou make,
When wert thou kind in anything?


" And how I quenchèd all thy care
Lift up thine eyes and thou mayst see:
My wounds, wet, bloody and bare
As I was wrought on the rood tree.
Thou seest me for default ill-fare
In sickness and in poverty,
Yet of thy goods thou wouldst not spare,
Nor once hast come to visit me.
All earthly things I gave to thee,
Both bird and beast and fowl flying;
And told thee how that charity
And mercy surpass everything."


These are the works of Mercy's word
By which Christ will us arraign,
That shall astonish with that word
All that treason might distrain.
But here unless we make us even
There may no might or gifts attain:
Then unto the King of Heaven
The Book says we shall say again:
"When hast thou, Lord, in prison lain?
When wert thou on the earth dwelling?
When saw we thee in any pain?
When asked thou us for anything? "

"When ye saw others blind and lame
That for my love asked you ought:
He that did it in my name
It was to me both deed and thought.
But ye that hated Christian men
And recked not ever for my wrath,
Your service shall be endless shame,
Hell fire that slaketh not.
And ye that with my blood I bought
And loved me even in your living,
Ye shall have that ye sought,
Mercy that passeth everything."


This time shall tide, it is no play,
And well for him that hath got grace
Pleasing to his God to pay
And mercy seek while he hath space!
For when our mouths are crammed with clay
And black worms our corpse embrace,
Then is too late, Man, in good fay,
To seek amends for thy trespass.
With meekness Heaven thou mayst purchase;
Other meed there thou canst not bring;
But know thy God in every case
And love him best of everything.


To God and man were holden best
To love, and his wrath eschew:
Nor is there so unkind a beast
That less does where is his due.
For beasts and fowls most and least
The course of nature all pursue;

And when we break so God's behest,
Against nature we are untrue.
For nature would that we him knew
And dread him most in our doing.
It is not right he us should rue,
For Mercy passeth everything.


Now harlotry for mirth we hold,
And virtue turneth unto vice,
And simony hath churches sold,
And law is waxen covetous.
Our faith is frail to twist and fold,
For truth is put at little price;
Our God is gluttony and gold,
Drunkenness, lechery and dice.
Lo, here our life and our device,
Our love, our lust and our liking;
Yet, if we will repent and rise,
Mercy surpasseth everything.


Unlustily our life we lead,
Manhood and we are torn in two:
To heaven nor hell we take no heed,
But one day come, another go.
Who is the master now but meed
And pride that wakened all our woe?
We stint neither for shame nor dread
To rend our God from top to toe.
There will no worship with us wake
Till Charity be made a king:
Then shall our sins 'minish and slake
And mercy surpass everything.

I say no more of this to you,
Although I could if that I would;
For ye have heard both why and how
Began this tale within that wood.
And this men know full well, I trow,
How that merlin's feet are cold,
How 'tis their make on bank and bough
A live bird in their claws to hold;
From foot to foot to flutter and fold
To keep them from slumbering;
As I a hawthorn can behold,
I saw myself the very thing.


When he had held it so all night,
On the morrow he let it away,
Whether gentry taught him so or not
I cannot tell you, in good fay!
But God, as Thou art full of might,
Though service to thee we do not pay,
Grant us repentance and respite,
And shrift and host on our last day:
As thou art God and man alway,
Thou be our help at our ending:
Before thy face that we may say:
"Now Mercy passeth everything."

Vernon MS., *c.* 1385


68

## DEO GRACIAS

IN a church where I could kneel,
This latter day at morning tide,
I liked the service wondrous well,
And for that liking did abide.
I saw a clerk a book forth bring
That prickèd was in many a place;
Fast he sought what he should sing,
And all was Deo Gracias.


All the choristers in that choir
On that word fast 'gan they cry;
The noise was good and I drew near,
And called a priest full privily
And said, "Sir, for your courtesy,
Tell me, if ye have a space,
What it meaneth and for why
Ye sing thus Deo Gracias?"


In silk that comely clerk was clad
And o'er a lectern leanèd he;
And with his word he made me glad,
And said, "Son, I will tell it thee:
Father and Son in Trinity,

The Holy Ghost, the ground of grace,
All so often thank do we
As we say Deo Gracias.


"To thank and bless Him we are bound
With all the mirths that we may mind;
For all the world in woe was wound
Till that He crept into our kind:
A lovesome lady He lit within,
The worthiest that ever was—
And shed His blood for our sin,
And therefore Deo Gracias."


Then said the priest, "Son, by thy leave,
I must set forth now service,
I pray thee take it not to grieve,
For thou hast heard all my device:
Because why, it is clerkly wise,
And Holy Church mood in her mass,
Unto the Prince of mickle prize
For to sing Deo Gracias."


Out of that church I made my way,
And on that word was all my thought,
And twenty times I 'gan to say,
"God grant that I forget it not."
Though I were out of goodhap brought,
What help to me to say "alas"?
In the name of God, whate'er be wrought,
I shall say Deo Gracias.

In mishap and in goodhap both,
That word is good to say or sing,
And not to wail or to be wrath,
Though all is not to our liking:
For grief will not for ever sting,
And sometime pleasure will overpass,
But aye in hope of amending,
I shall say Deo Gracias.


Amend what thou hast done amiss,
And do well then and have no dread,
Whether so thou be in bale or bliss,
Good sufferance will get thee meed;
If thou thy life in liking lead,
Look thou be kind in every case;
Thank thy God if well thou speed
With this word Deo Gracias.


If God hath given thee virtues more
Than He hath to other two or three,
Then I rede thee rule thee so
That men may speak worship of thee.
Be feared of pride and boasting flee,
Thy virtues let no filth deface,
But keep thee clean, courteous and free,
And think on Deo Gracias.


If thou art made an officer,
And art a man of mickle might,
What cause thou deem'st, look it be clear,
And reive thee from no man his right.
If thou art strong and fierce of fight,

For envy ne'er a man give chase,
But dread thy God both day and night,
And think on Deo Gracias.

If we this word in heart will have,
All days in love and loyalty spend,
Of Christ by covenant we may crave
That joy shall never have an end,
Out of this world when we shall wend,
Into His palace for to pass,
And sit among His kindly saints,
And there sing Deo Gracias.

Vernon MS., c. 1385

# THIS WORLD FARES BUT AS A FANTASY

I WOULD I knew of some wise wight
   Truthfully what this world were;
It fareth as a fowl in flight,
Now it is hence, now it is here;
Nor be we ever so full of might,
Now sit we high, now lie low on bier;
And be we never so brave and right,
Now we be sick, now of good cheer,
Now is one proud without a peer,
Now the one we count nothing by;
And whoso will think heartily here,
This world fares but as a fantasy.

The course, as well we ken, of the sun
Ariseth east and goeth down west;
The rivers into the sea they run
And it is never the more possessed;
Winds rush here and hence again,
In snow or rain is no arrest;
When this will stay who wots or when
Save only God, on ground that goest?
The earth in one is ever pressed,
Now all dripping, now all dry;
But each man glides forth as a guest:
This world fares but as a fantasy.

Kindreds come and kins have gone,
As joinèd generations;
But all hence passeth, every one,
For all their preparations;
Some are forgotten clean and good
Among all manner of nations,
So shall men think nothing of us foregone,
Who now have occupations:
And all these same disputations
Idly all of us occupy;
For Christ He maketh His creations,
And this world fares as a fantasy.

Which is man, who knows or what,
Whether that he be aught or naught?
Of Earth and Air grows up a gnat,
And so doth man when all is sought;
Though man be waxen great and fat,
Man melts away as doth a moth.
Man's might is hardly worth a mat,
That angers himself and turns to naught.
Who knows, save He that all hath wrought,
What man becometh when he shall die?
Who knows by death ought profit be bought?
For this world fares as a fantasy.

Dieth man, and beasts die,
And all is one occasion;
And all one death who all doth drive,
And have one incarnation,
Save that man is the more sly,
All is a comparison.

Who knows if man's soul goeth on high
And that the beasts' souls sink down?
Who knoweth beasts' intention,
On their Creator how they cry
Save only God that knoweth their tone?
For this world fares as a fantasy.


Each sect hopeth itself to save
Boldly by their own belief;
And each on God doth cry and crave—
Why should God with them have grief?
Upon truth they rend and rave
And each one choseth God for chief,
And hope in God each one they have
And by their wit their working preach.
Thus many matters with men move
Searching their wits how and why;
But God's mercy us all behoves:
For this world fares as a fantasy.


For thus men stumble and sear their wit
And move matters many and fell,
Some believe on him and some on it,
As children learning how to spell.
But none seeth one abides a bit
When quietly death will on him steal;
For He that high in heaven doth sit,
He is our help and hope of heal;
For woe's the end of the world's weal—
Each life look where I may lie—
This world is false, fickle and frail
And fareth but as a fantasy.

Wherefore will we for to know
The pointings of God's privacy?
More than He listeth for to show,
We should not know in no degree;
An idle boast it is to blow
As master in divinity.
Think that we live on earth below
And God on high in majesty;
Of material mortality
We meddle without mastery.
The more we trace the Trinity,
The more we fall in fantasy.

But leave we our disputation,
Believe on Him that all hath wrought;
We may not prove by any reason
How He was born that all hath bought;
But whole in our intention,
Worship we Him in heart and thought,
For He may turn kinds upside down
That all kinds made out of naught.
When all our books have been forth brought,
And all our craft of clergy,
And all our wits been thoroughly sought,
Yet we fare but as a fantasy.

Of fantasy is all our fare,
Old and young and all of us here;
But make we merry and slay care
And worship we God while we are here;
Spend our goods and little spare
And each man cherish other's cheer.
Think how we came hither all bare,

And in doubt our wending where—
Pray we the Prince that hath no peer
Take us wholly to His mercy,
And keep us in our conscience clear,
For this world is but a fantasy.

By example men may see,
A great tree groweth out of the ground;
Nothing abated the earth will be
Though it be great and huge and round.
Right there will be rooted the same tree
When eld hath made his kind unsound,
Though there were rotted many a tree
The earth will not increase a pound.
Thus waxeth and waneth man, horse and hound,
From naught to naught thus hence we hie;
And we stay but a brief ground,
For this world is but a fantasy.

Vernon MS., c. 1385

# MANE NOBISCUM DOMINE

IN summer, ere the Ascension,
  At evensong on a Sunday,
Dwelling in my devotion
For the peace fast 'gan I pray;
I heard a reason for my pay
That written was with words three,
And thus it is shortly to say:
Mane nobiscum Domine!


What this word doth surely mean
In English tongue I shall you tell;
In our conscience an we be clean
Deign thee, Lord, with us to dwell—
The fiend's assault is fierce and fell—
Who for us died upon the tree,
In wit and worship, woe and well,
Mane nobiscum Domine!


When Thou from death wast risen and gone,
Then as a palmer forth thou passed,
So metst thou pilgrims, making moan,
But yet they wittest not who thou wast.

Thus then asketh Cleophas:
"The night is nigh, as we may see,
The light of day is waxen less;
Mane nobiscum Domine!"


Dwell with us, our Father dear,
Thy biding is in heaven's bliss,
And ever thy name be hallowed here;
Thy kingdom let us never miss.
In heaven thy will fulfillèd is
And here on earth that so it be,
The right ways that thou wouldst us wis,
Mane nobiscum Domine!


Our bread, our each day's daily food,
Lord God dear for us dight.
Our debts, God, that art so good,
Forgive us with thy mickle might,
As we will them, with hearts light,
That in our debt or danger be;
Lest we rule us not aright,
Mane nobiscum Domine!


Lord, dwell with us, in all our need,
Without thee we have got no might
Our hands to raise for our own need,
Nor wit nor will nor saving sight.
In any case, if we are fraught,
We cannot but we cry to thee:
In all our need both day and night,
Mane nobiscum Domine!

Who dwell with thee need have no doubt
For neither sin nor sudden chance.
But aye the fiend is close about
To put us, Lord, from thy pleasance;
When we are out of governance,—
Our flesh is frail, we cannot flee,—
Keep us from all cumberance,
Mane nobiscum Domine!


Dwell with us, Lord of love and peace,
Make thine abiding us within,
In charity that we increase,
And keep us out of deadly sin.
Turn never thy face away from us,
For Mary's love, that maiden free;
When we shall any work begin,
Mane nobiscum Domine!


Mane nobiscum Domine!
Withouten thee we be right nought.
What joy or bliss were that to thee
To lose that thou hast dearly bought?
In word, in will, in heart and thought,
So pray we to the Trinity:
Out of this world when we are brought,
Mane nobiscum Domine!

Vernon MS., *c.* 1385

# AGAINST MY WILL I TAKE MY LEAVE

NOW, sirs and ladies, bold and blythe,
   To bless you here now am I bound;
To thank you all a thousand times
And pray God save you whole and sound:
Wherever ye go on grass or ground,
He you govern and never grieve:
For friendship that I here have found,
Against my will I take my leave.

For friendship and for gifts of good,
For meat and drink in great plenty,
That Lord was wrought upon the rood
Keep He this goodly company:
On sea or land where that ye be,
Govern He you and never grieve:
Such good disport ye have made for me,
Against my will I take my leave.

Against my will although I wend,
I may not always tarry here:
For everything shall have an end,
Friends are not always in good cheer.
Be we never so lief and dear,
From this world all shall take their leave,
And when we busk us to our bier,
Against our will we take our leave.

And wend we shall, I wot not when
Nor whitherward that we shall fare:
To endless bliss or endless pain,
And everyman is markèd there.
For this I rede each man beware
And let our works our words receive,
So that no sin our souls forefare
When that our life hath ta'en his leave.


When that our life his leave hath ta'en,
Our body lies bounded by the wall:
Our riches all from us are reft,
Into cold clots our corse shall fall.
Where are thy friends, how wilt thou know?
Let him who will his soul relieve!
I rede thee, man, ere thou lie low,
Be ready aye to take thy leave.


Be ready aye, whate'er befall,
All suddenly lest He indite:
Thou wott'st not when thy Lord will call,
Look that thy lamp be burning bright;
Believe me well, but thou hast light,
Coldly thy Lord will thee receive,
And cast thee far from out His sight,
For all too late thou tookst thy leave.


Now God that maid in Bethlehem bore,
Give us His grace to serve Him so,
That we may come His face before,
Out of this world when we shall go;

And to amend what we misdo,
In clay ere that we cling and cleave,
And make us even with friend and foe,
And in good time to take our leave.


Now have good day, ye good men all,
Have ye good day, both young and old,
Have ye good day, both great and small,
And gramercy a thousand-fold!
If ever I might, full fain I would,
Do ought that were unto your leave:
Christ keep you out of care and cold,
For now 'tis time I take my leave.

Vernon MS., c. 1385

# CHRISTMAS NIGHT

JESU my sweet Son dear,
  On a poor bed Thou liest here,
That grieves me sore:
Thy cradle bare is as a bier,
Ox and ass Thy fellows here,
Weep may I therefore!


Jesu, sweet Son, be not wrath
Though I have neither clout nor cloth
Round Thee to fold;
I have no clout Thee to nest,
But lay Thy feet to my breast
And keep Thee from the cold.

                    Harl. MS., *c.* 1375

## SAINT STEPHEN

SAINT STEPHEN was a clerk in King Herod's
hall,
And served him with bread and cloth, as to a king befall.


Stephen from the kitchen came, with a boar's head in
his hand;
He saw a star was fair and bright over Bethlehem stand.


He cast down the boar's head and went into the hall.
"I forsake thee, King Herod, and thy works all.


"I forsake thee, King Herod, and thy works all:
There is a child in Bethlehem is better than us all."


"What aileth thee, Stephen? What is this doth befall?
Lacked to thee either meat or drink in King Herod's
hall?"


"Lacked me neither meat nor drink in King Herod's
hall:
There is a child in Bethlehem born is better than we
all."

"What aileth thee, Stephen? Art thou mad or wouldst
thou breed?
Lacked to thee either gold or fee or any rich weed?"


"Lacked to me neither gold nor fee nor any rich weed:
There is a child in Bethlehem born shall help us at our
need."

"This is all sooth, Stephen, all so sooth I wis,
As that this capon crow shall, lies here in my dish."


That word was not so soon said, that word in that hall,
The capon crowed "Christus natus est" among the
lords all.

"Rise up, rise, my tormentors, rouse ye and all at one,
And lead Stephen out of the town and stone him with
stones."

Took they Stephen and stoned him in the way;
And therefore is his Even on Christ's own Day.

15th cent.

# RATS AWAY!

I COMMAND all ye rattens that here be about,
That none dwell in this place, nor within, nor with-
    out,
By the virtue of Jesus Christ that Mary bore about,
To whom all creatures ought to lout,
And through the virtues of Mark, Matthew, Luke and
    John—
All four evangels according as one—
Through the virtue of St. Gertrude that maid clean,
    God grant the grace
    That no rat dwell in the place
That her name is named in;
And through the virtue of St. Kasi,
That holy man that prayed to God Almighty
From wrongs they wrought in
His mede and his bin,
By day and by night,
God bade them flee and be gone out of every man's
    sight!
Dominus Deus Sabaoth! Emmanuel, the great God's
    name!
I command go as fast as ye can, ye rats and all other
    shame!
God save the place from all other wicked wights
Both by days and by nights!
In Nomine Patris et Filius et Spiritus Sancti.
                          Amen.

                    Rawl. MS., 14th cent.

# EARTH UPON EARTH

## I

EARTH out of earth is wonderfully wrought:
Earth from earth hath got dignity of naught.
Earth upon earth hath set all his thought
How that earth upon earth may be high brought.

Earth upon earth would be a high king;
But how earth shall to earth thinketh he no thing.
When earth biddeth earth his rents home to bring,
Then shall earth out of earth have a piteous parting.

Earth upon earth winneth castles and towers;
Then saith earth to earth "This is all ours."
When earth upon earth hath built up his bowers
Then shall earth upon earth suffer sharp showers.

Earth upon earth, even as mould on mould,—
So goeth earth upon earth all glittering in gold;
Even as earth upon earth never go should,
And yet shall earth unto earth sooner than he would.

## II

Oh, thou wretched earth that on earth travailest night
and day
To flourish with thine earth, to paint earth with wanton
array,
Yet shalt thou earth, for all thine earth, makest thou it
never so quaint and gay,
Out of this earth into the earth, there to cling a clot of
clay.


Oh, wretched man, why art thou proud, that art of earth
makèd?
Hither broughtest thou no shroud, but poor camest thou
and naked.
When thy soul is gone out and thy body in earth rakèd,
Then thy body that was rank and undevout is of all men
hated.


Out of this earth came to this earth this wretch's gar-
ment,
To hide his earth, to lap this earth, to him was clothing
lent.
Now goeth earth upon earth rueful, ragged and rent;
Therefore shall earth under earth suffer long torment.


Why that earth too much love earth, wondering I think;
Or why earth for superfluous earth so sore will sweat
and swink;
For when that earth upon the earth is brought unto the
brink,
Then shall earth upon earth ruefully think.

# III

Lo! earth upon earth consider ye may,
How earth cometh into earth, naked in every way.
Why should earth upon earth go now so stout or gay
When earth shall pass out from earth in so poor array?


Would God, therefore, this earth, while that he is on
earth, to this would his mind bring,
How that earth out of the earth shall have his again-
rising;
And this earth for this earth shall yield straight reckon-
ing.
Should never then this earth for this earth misplease
heaven's King.


Therefore, thou earth upon earth that so wickedly hast
wrought,
While that thou earth art upon earth, turn again thy
thought,
And pray to that God upon earth that all the earth hath
wrought,
That thou earth upon earth to bliss may be brought.


O Thou Lord, that madest this earth for this earth and
suffered here pain's ill,
Let never this earth for this earth come to grief or spill,
But that this earth upon this earth be ever working thy
will,
So that this earth from this earth may go up to thine
high hill!

Lambeth MS., c. 1430

## TESTAMENTUM DOMINI

WIT ye well, all that be here,
    And after shall be live and dear,
That I, Jesu of Nazareth,
For love of man have suffered death,
Upon a cross, with wounds five,
While I was man, on earth alive.
I have given and made a grant
To all that ask it penitent,
Heaven's bliss, without ending,
As long as I thereof am King.
Keep I no more, for all pains' smart,
Except the true love of man's heart,
And that thou be in charity
And love thy neighbour as I do thee.
This is the rent thou shalt give me
As to the chief lord of thy fee.

If any man now would say,
I have not died for men's pay,
Rather than man should be forlorn,
Yet once again I would be torn.

Witness the day that turned to night,
And the sun withdrew his light:
Witness the earth that then did quake,

The stones that all in pieces brake:
Witness the veil in two did rive,
And dead men that rose up alive:
Witness my Mother and Saint John,
And there were many another one.

It witness of this very thing,
Myself as seal thereto I bring.
This was given at Calvary,
The first day of the great Mercy.

Ash. MS., 15th cent.

## VENI CORONABERIS

*A song of great sweetness from Christ to his dear Dame*

SURGE mea sponsa, sweet in sight,
And see thy son, thou gavest suck to, shine:
Thou shalt abide with thy babe so bright,
Be called a queen in glory mine.
Thy breasts, mother, full well I mind
I had to my meat that I might not miss,
Above all creatures, my mother kind,
Veni coronaberis.

Come cleaner than crystal to my cage,
Columba mea, I thee call;
And see thy son that in servitude
For men's souls was made a thrall.
In thine inner chamber so principal
Privily played I without amiss;
Mine high seat, mother, have thou shall;
Veni coronaberis.

For macula, mother, was never in thee,
Filia Sion, thou art the flower:
Full sweetly shalt thou sit by me
And bear a crown in mine high tower;

And all my saints to thine honour
Shall honour thee, mother, in my bliss,
That blessèd body that bare me in bower:
Veni coronaberis.


Tota pulchra art thou to my pleasing,
My mother, princess of paradise!
A well filled with water from thee 'gan spring
Whereby shall all my righteous rise:
The well of mercy in thee, mother, lies
To bring thy blessèd body to bliss;
And my saints shall serve thee with happy cries:
Veni coronaberis.


Veni electa mea, my mother sweet!
When thou badest me, babe, be full still
Full goodly then our lips would meet
As branches with blossoms bright on a hill:
Favus distillans, it went with a will
From our lips when we did kiss:
Therefore, mother, now, full still,
Veni coronaberis.


Veni de Libano, thou lovely in launch,
That lapped me lovely with liking song,
Thou shalt abide with a blessèd branch
That so seemly of thy body sprung:
Ego, flos campi, thy flower was sold,
That on Calvary cried to thee, I wis:
Mother, thou knowest this is as I told:
Veni coronaberis.

Pulchra ut luna, thou bearest the light,
As the sun that shinest clear:
Veni in ortum meum, thou daintiest dam,
To smell my spices that crowd forth here.
My palace is dight for thy pleasure clear,
Full of bright branches and blossoms of bliss;
Come now, mother, to thy darling dear:
Veni coronaberis!


Quid est ista, so virtuous,
That is everlasting for her meekness?
Aurora consurgens gracious,
So benign a lady and of such brightness?
This is the colour of kind clearness,
Regina coeli, that ne'er did amiss.
Here endeth the high song of great sweetness.
Veni coronaberis.

Lambeth MS., c. 1430

# RICHARD DE CASTRE'S PRAYER TO JESUS

JESUS, Lord, that madest me
    And with thy blessèd blood hast bought,
Forgive that I have grievèd thee
With word, with will, and eke with thought.

Jesus, in whom is all my trust,
That died upon the rood tree,
Withdraw mine heart from fleshly lust
And from all worldly vanity.

Jesus, for thy four wounds' smart
On thy feet and thy hands two,
Make me meek and low of heart
And thee to love as I should do!

Jesus, for thy bitter wound
Went to thy heart's root innerly,
For sin that hath mine heart held bound,
Thy blessèd blood be remedy!

And, Jesus Christ, to thee I call,
Thou art God, full of might,
Keep me clean that I do not fall
In deadly sin nor day nor night.

Jesus, grant me mine asking,
Perfect patience in my decease,
And never might I do that thing
Should thee in any wise displease.


Jesus, for the deadly tears
That thou sheddest for my guilt,
Hear and speed my prayers
And spare me that I be not spilt.


Jesus, for them I thee beseech
That anger thee in any wise,
Withhold from them thine hand of wrath,
And let them live in thy service.


Jesus, most comfort for to see
Of all thy saints every one,
Comfort them that are full of care,
And help them that are woebegone.


Jesus, keep them that are good,
And amend them that have grieved thee,
And send them fruits of earthly food
As each man needeth in his degree.


Jesus, that art withouten lies,
Almighty God in trinity,
Cease these wars and send us peace
With lasting love and charity.

Jesus, that art the corner-stone
Of all holy church in middle earth,
Bring thy folds and flocks in one,
And rule them rightly with one herd.


Jesus, for thy blessed blood,
Bring, if thou wilt, those souls to bliss
From whom I have had any good,
And spare what they have done amiss.

Amen.

Lambeth MS., c. 1430

## "THIS LITTLE BILL"

MY heart's joy, the whole of all my pleasure,
   Whom that I serve and shall do in faith duly
With true intent and humble observance
You for to please in that that I can truly,
Beseeching you, this little bill and I
May heartily with some happiness and fear,
Be recommended most especially
To you, the flower of living beauty clear!

And if ye list to have knowledge of my part;
I am in health, God's thanks that so it be,
As to my body, but truly not in heart
Nor shall be till that time I may you see;
But think that I as truly will be he
That for your ease will do my power and might,
Be your defence in all adversity,
As though that you were daily in my sight.

I write no more to you for lack of space,
But I beseech the Holy Trinity
You save and keep, supported by His grace
Be your defence in all adversity.
Go, little bill, and say thou wert with me
Even this same day at mine up-rising,
When that I then besought of God's mercy
To have my sovereign thus ever in His keeping.

Likewise as God me save
So am I only yours,
What pain so ever I have,
And will be at all hours.

                              Lambeth MS., *c.* 1430

# DO MERCY BEFORE THY JUDGEMENT

THERE is no creator but One,
    Maker of every creature,
God alone and ever one,
The Three-in-One aye to endure.
To that Lord we make our moan,
In Whom all comfort is and cure;
To think how frail we be, each one,
In this world, a hard aventure;
Whoso thereof is most assured,
Soonest he shall be shamed and bent:
Ere Thou the world with fire make pure,
Do Mercy before Thy Judgement!

We ask for mercy ere Thou judge,
Lest Thou damn that that Thou hast wrought:
What joy were it the fiend to please,
To give him that that Thou hast bought?
And from Thy sight if Thou us drive,
We were but lost, right as nought:
Now make us like to Thee alive;
In love and dread set Thou our thought!
Sin hath so thoroughly through us sought
There is no trust in our intent:
Unto account ere we be brought,
Do Mercy before Thy Judgement!

For Thou hast bidden us ask and have;
Thou givest mercy when we call;
Thou hast ordainèd man to save
Mercy above Thy workings all.
Also heart's blood for us Thou gave,
To make us free that erst were thrall:
Let never the devil that soul deprave
That washed was in Thy holy well.
Our flesh is frail, that maketh us fall,
With grace we rise and should repent,
And thus we hope that thus we shall
Have Mercy before Thy Judgement.

We ask for mercy by each thing,
For Thou art kind in each degree:
Thou gave us with stones a beginning,
And with Thy spirit endowed us free:
With trees Thou gave us a growing,
With beasts feeling life have we;
With angels understanding,
With belief wedded unto Thee;
And with Thy blood bought are we:
Yet we are false and negligent:
We can nor climb away nor flee
Thy Mercy or Thy Judgement!

Wherefore our spirits and our life,
Into Thy hands we thus betake;
Out of temptations, out of strife,
To save us when we sleep or wake.
Now Jesu for Thy wounds five,
And also for Thy Mother's sake,
The devil away from us drive

When death shall o'er us mastery make!
Thou saidst Thou wouldst us not forsake
When Thou upon the rood wert rent:
Against Thy Doom we cry and quake:
Do Mercy before Thy Judgement!

And if Thou deem us rightfully,
Give Mercy execution;
And if we have served Thee unkindly,
Take heed to our intention.
We yield us sinful and sorry,
With knowledge and contrition;
Our baptism and Thy mercy
We take to our protection.
Belief is our salvation,
By law of Thy commandment;
Now Christ put all Thy Passion
Betwixt us and Thy Judgement!

Wheatley MS., 15th cent.<br>Lambeth MS., c. 1430

# AVE MARIA!

HAIL to thee, Mary, thou Mother of Christ,
Hail the most blessèd that ever bare child;
Hail that conceivèd all in love
The Son of God, both meek and mild:
Hail Maiden sweet that was ne'er defiled,
Hail well of wit and of wisdom,
Hail thou flower! Thou fairest in field,
Ave Regina Coelorum!

Hail comely queen, comfort of care,
Hail blessèd lady, both fair and bright;
Hail thee, salver of all sores,
Hail thou lamp of gentlest light!
Hail blessèd burd in whom Christ was dight,
Hail joy of men both all and some,
Hail pinnacle in heaven's height,
Mater Regis angelorum!

Hail crownèd queen, fairest of all,
Hail, all our bliss within thee bred;
Hail, that all women on thee call
In time when they are hard bestèd;
Hail thou that all the fiend-kin dread,
And shall do till the day of doom!
With maiden-milk thy Son thou fed,
O Maria flos virginum!

Hail the fairest that ever God found,
Who chose thee for His own bower,
Hail thou lantern for ever alight,
To thee shall lout both rich and poor;
Hail spice, the sweetest of savour,
Hail, whence all our joyings come,
Hail of all women fruit and flower,
Velud rosa vel lilium!

Hail to thee, goodly ground of grace,
Hail blessèd star upon the sea;
Hail comforter in every case,
Hail thee, chiefest in charity;
Hail well of wit and of mercy,
Hail that bare Jesus God's own Son,
Hail tabernacle of the Trinity:
Fundes preces ad filium!

Hail to thee, virgin of all virgins,
Hail blessèd Mother! Hail blessèd May!
Hail nourisher of sweet Jesus,
Hail chiefest of chastity, sooth to say:
Lady, keep us in our last day
That we may to thy kingdom come:
For me and for all Christians pray,
Pro saluta fidelium.

Lambeth MS., c. 1430

# NOEL!

NOW be glad
And not sad,
For Verbum Caro Factum est.

This may I prove without a let,
When Gabriel our Lady met,
On his knee he him set
                    So mildly:
"Thou shalt conceive this very day
                    Salvator Mundi."

A star shone, through God, his grace,
As God's own will it was;
The shepherds saw in that place
                    Angels two,
And they among them sang a song
                    Gloria in excelsis Deo!

The child was born upon Yule day,
As prophets to us 'gan say:
His Mother sang lullay, lullay,
                    Into the east:
Therefore mankind without an end
                    Sing Verbum Caro Factum est.

And then by token of a star,
Three kings there came from far,
And offered frankincense and myrrh
        To Christ so free:
Then they said with merry cheer,
        Mane nobiscum Domine.


Therefore pray we, every one,
To the bairn that then was born,
He save us from all sin and scorn
        In peace and rest:
And all mankind without an end
        Sing Verbum Caro Factum est!

        15th cent.

# A GREETING ON NEW YEAR'S MORNING

PRECIOUS jewel can I find none to sell
 To send you, my sovereign, this New Year's
  Morrow,
Wherefore for lack and for a hansel good
Mine heart I send you; and wish from St. John to borrow
That an hundred years without adversity or sorrow
You may live. I pray to God so may you be,
And all of your desires to send you speedily!

Beseeching you, dear, as entirely as I can,
To take in grace this poor gift, only for my sake;
As is the custom and has been many a New Year's Day
Each friend to one another give gifts and take;
Rich is it not, nor worth great boast to make
Save a heart that is remembering you in every scene;
That was pierced once, the wound is yet green.

That it is yours, truly, it is my thought;
My possession and my part therein I deny:
And, touching that old word of "had I wist,"
Unto my life's end fully I it defy.
Palamon gave his heart to Emily;
He vouched it no better nor repented it less
Than I do this gift, God take I to witness!

My purpose hath been long my heart so to send
But till this New Year's Day I durst not for shame.
Men say there is no thing so free as a gift,
And if I take it back I were fully to blame.
But as in that default I will not lose my name,
So that that I give once is given for ever more.
For thus have love and truth learned me their lore;
    Evermore and without change for ever
     Till body and soul part and dissever.

Lambeth MS., c. 1430

# THE TWELVE DAYS OF CHRISTMAS

THE first day of Yule have we in mind
   How God was man born of our kind,
For He the binding would unbind
       Of all our sin and weakness.

The second day we sing of Stephen
Who stonèd was and went up even
To God that he saw stand in heaven
       And crowned was for his prowess.

The third day 'longeth to Saint John,
That was Christ's darling, dearer none,
Whom He bequeathed when He was gone,
       His Mother dear for her clearness.

The fourth day, of the children young
That Herod to death did do with wrong,
And Christ they could not tell with tongue
       But with their blood bore witness.

The fifth 'longeth to Saint Thomas,
That as a strong pillar of brass
Held up the church, and slain he was
       For he stood with righteousness.

The eighth day Jesus took His name
That saved the world from sin and shame,
Was circumcisèd for no blame
        But for example of His meekness.


The twelfth day offered the kings three
Gold, myrrh and incense, these gifts free,
For God and man and king was He;
        Thus worshipped they His worthiness.


On the fortieth day came Mary mild
Unto the Temple with her Child,
To show her clean, was ne'er defiled,
        And therewith endeth Christmas.

                     15th cent.

## PILGRIMS AT SEA

### *Or the pleasures of the voyage*

MEN may leave all games
    That sail unto Saint James,
For many a man it shames
    When they begin to sail:
For when they have taken to the sea,
At Sandwich or at Winchelsea,
At Bristol or where it may be,
    Their hearts begin to fail.
Anon, the master commandeth fast
To his shipmen, with all haste,
To dress them soon about the mast,
    Their tacklings to take.
With "Howe! hissa!" then they cry:
"What ho! mate, thou standest too nigh,
Thy fellow may not hale thee by."
    Thus they their shouting make.
A boy or twain anon go up high,
And over athwart the sailyard lie—
"Y how! Talia!" the remnant cry
    And pull with all their might.
"Bestow the boat, boatswain, anon,
That our pilgrims may play thereon:
For some are like to cough and groan
    Or it be full midnight."

"Hale the bowline! Now veer the sheet—
Cook, make ready anon our meat,
Our pilgrims have no lust to eat,
    I pray God give them rest."
"Go to the helm! What ho! So near?
Steward, fellow! A pot of beer!"
"Ye shall have it, sir, with a good cheer
    Anon, all of the best."
"Hilho! Trussa! Haul on the brails!
Thou haul'st not! By God, he fails,
Oh see how well our good ship sails!"
    And thus they say among.
"Hail in the wartack!" "It shall be done."
"Steward, cover the board anon,
And set bread and salt thereon,
    And tarry not too long."
Then cometh one and saith, "Be merry:
Ye shall have a storm or a skerry."
"Hold thou thy peace! thou canst not wherry,
    Ye change colour wondrous sore!"
This meanwhile the pilgrims lie,
And have their bowls fast them bye,
And cry after hot malvoisie
    "To help them and restore."
And some would have a salted toast,
For they might eat nor boiled nor roast;
A man might soon pay for their cost,
    For one day as for twain.
Some laid their books upon their knee,
And read so long they might not see—
"Alas! mine head will cleave in three!"
    One crieth out, certain.
Then comes our owner, like a lord,
And speaketh many a royal word,

And dresses himself to the high board,
    To see all things be well.
Anon he calleth a carpenter
And biddeth him bring with him his gear,
To make the cabins here and there,
    With many a feeble cell;
A sack of straw were there right good,
For some must lap them in their hood:
I had as lief be in the wood,
    Without or meat or drink:
For when that we should go to bed,
The pump was nigh to our bed head;
A man he were as good as dead
    As smell thereof or think!

            Trin. Coll. MS., 15th cent.

## "O MIGHTY LADY"

O MIGHTY Lady, our leading, to have
In heaven our abiding,
To the feast everlasting,
Is set a Branch us to bring!

You won this with bliss, the blessing of God
For your good bearing,
Where you bent for your winning;
Since queen, and your son is King!

Our forefathers' father, our feeding, our pope,
At your breast, a suckling:
In heaven's bliss, I beg this thing,
Attendance without ending.

We have seen the bright queen with cunning and bliss
The Blossom-fruit bearing:
I would, as I could, sing,
Win your love, in your loving.

Queen chosen of God, our guiding Mother,
Maiden notwithstanding,
Who wed with such a rich ring
As God would the good wedding:

Help us, pray for us, proffering our souls,
Assoil at our ending:
Make all that fall to us bring
Your Son's life, our sins leaving!

So we may the day of dying receive
Our houseling;
As He may take us, waking,
To Him, 'neath His mighty wing.

                    Hengwrt MS., 15th cent.

## TO MY LADY DEAR

FRESH flower of womanly nature,
    Ye be full gentle, a goodly one to see,
And all so stedfast as any creature
That is living in any degree.
Fulfilled with all benignity,
An ensample of all worthiness,
To them that of you have necessity
Be gracious ever in your gentleness.


But I am so bound, I can make no start,
To you complaining in this mannèr
Beseeching you ever with mine whole heart:
And humbly also I of you require,
As an only one, without a peer
Of lovelihead and of assurance,
I that am yours, be ye far or near,
Cast me not out from your remembrance!


Consider, dear lady, of your pity
The high complaint of my disease,
My grief and mine adversity!
Ye be my healing may me best please.
Show me your sweet soul in my disease

For other lover have I none.
And ever I will be ready you to please,
Never any to have but you alone.


None but you, lady and mistress,
From whose heart in life mine may not dissever.
So fast is it lockèd in the lock of stedfastness
That in your service it shall abide for ever.
You wit well my woe you may recover,
My pain relieve may none but ye,
My death and life lieth in you ever
Right as it pleaseth you to save or to flee.


Loathe to offend. So I may my lady please,
Welcome pain and fie on ease!

Lambeth MS, c. 1430

# A PRAISING OF WOMEN

I AM as light as any roe,
To praise women wherever I go.


To mispraise women it were a shame,
For a woman was thy dame;
Our blessed Lady beareth the name
    Of all women wherever they go.


A woman is a worthy thing.
They do the wash and do the wring,
"Lullay! Lullay!" she doth to thee sing,
    And yet she has but care and woe.


A woman is a worthy wight,
She serveth a man both day and night;
Thereto she putteth all her might;
    And yet she hath but care and woe.

Harl. MS., 15th cent.

# FILIUS REGIS MORTUUS EST ET RESUREXIT

## I

AS reason ruled my reckless mind,
 By wild ways wandering as I went,
A solemn city me fortuned to find:
To turn thereto was my intent.
A lovely lady, a maiden kind,
I met there mourning; but what she meant
I could not know; but fast she pined,
She swooned, she said, and was near forespent.
That blessed burd from the ground I raised,
With water I washed her face and breast:
Her hair, her face, she beat and rent,
Cried "Filius Regis mortuus est!


"The King's son," she said, "is dead,
The joy, the substance of my life!
The mother to see her own son bleed,
It cuts my heart as with a knife!
My son that I was wont to feed,
To lull, to lap with singing rife,—
Out of his heart the blood is shed,

Makes me his mother in much strife!
I am both maiden, mother, wife,
And sons have no more to suck my breast;
I may make sorrow without relief,
Filius Regis mortuus est!


"This Filius Regis, mine own dear child,
Hangs on the cross: I stand and see
How he is wounded and defiled
With spittings and spears so piteously.
I cried on him as I were wild,
'My sweet son dear, seest thou not me
Thine own dear mother?' He me beheld,
Said 'Mourn not, mother; thy sorrow let be.
I shall be thine and come to thee.'
He spake, I swooned: I never ceased.
Ah! Son, my son upon a tree!
Filius Regis mortuus est!


"He dieth, he dieth that is my bliss:
He sweat, he swooned, I cried alas!
No wonder is my great heaviness!
My father, my brother, my spouse he was,
My mother, my succour, and all that is!
Now fatherless, motherless, I may forth pass,
Brotherless, spouseless, full wretched, I wis,
As a thing forsaken that no thing hath!
Ah! Gabriel, thou called me full of grace,—
Nay full of sorrow thou seest my breast;
The tears run trickling down my face,
Filius Regis mortuus est.

"I looked up," she said, "unto my child:
I cried on the Jews that bade him hang.
The mother by the son was never defiled.
O death, death, thou doest me wrong!
My babe thou slayest, that never was wild;
Come slay the mother! Why tarry so long?
Thou murderous man, why art thou mild
Unto the mother would suffer long?
Thou pinest my son with pain strong:
Pine then the mother at my request!
Alas, I may sing a sorrowful song
Filius Regis mortuus est.


"Ah! Earth, 'gainst thee I claim appeal,
Thou that receivest his guiltless blood!
Thou stone! Why wouldst thou be so frail,
To be the mortise where the cross stood?
He made ye earth and stones to feel,
And ye be instruments now to the rood,
Ye slay your maker! Ye wit full well
He did never evil but evermore good.
He was ever meek and mild of mood;
Now is he stuck as he were a beast!
Alas, my babe, my living's food,
Filius Regis mortuus est!


"Thou tree, thou cross, how darest thou be
A gallows to hang thy maker so?
To his Father I appeal from thee,
That would be cause of my son's woe!
No cause, but help he died on thee!
Ye trees, cry mercy, ye are my foe!

Had ye ordained a cross for me,
To hang me by him, well had been so!
But what may I say? Where can I go?
Thou tree hast hanged a king, a priest,
Of all kings such there is no more,—
Filius Regis mortuus est.


"O ye creatures unkind! Thou iron, thou steel!
O thou sharp thorn! . . .
How dare ye slay your own best friend,
The holiest child that ever was born?
Ye have him wounded, ye have him pined;
Spear and nail his body have shorn!
Thou spear, why bore you the smith should grind
So sharp, that all his heart thou hast torn?
I may cry on thee even and morn,
A stainless maiden's son thou slayst!
I wring, I weep as a thing forlorn!
Filius Regis mortuus est!


"Now mortuus est my fairest lord!
Now dead is my dear child, alas!
Now I may walk about this world
As a wretch that wanteth grace!
All this I say to bear record;
No longer might I look on his face!
Thus come I from Calvary-ward,
Weeping and wailing that born I was.
If any love me, leave me a place
Where I may weep my fill and rest;
And my son will grant him some that he hath:
Filius Regis mortuus est."

## II

Why died thy son, thou maiden chaste?
The Second Person, and the Godhead not?
Nor the Third Person, the Holy Ghost:
This maketh me marvel much in my thought.
Since wisdom by the Son was taught,
When Adam into sin was brought,—
Three for three that we trespass not,—
Redemption's maker ere we were wrought.
Adam in a tree his hands had caught:
Christ's hands unto a tree were fast.
To fell our foe our friend hath fought,
And Filius Regis mortuus est.

"Go look," she said, "whilst thou mayst see,
I may no longer tarry from town."
I took my way up to the tree,
There the blood was running down.
Three days I dight me there to be
For pity of his passion:
He went to his grave alone from me.
Three women met I in procession.
I asked them whither they were bound;
They took full sorrow, without a rest,
Yet answered they with doleful sound,
Filius Regis mortuus est.

So to his grave I went aright,
And pursued after to wit the end;
I saw angels with great light
And seraphim's order adown descend.
The women they sobbed and mourned, sore in sight;
They said, "We laid him here with our hands."

The angel answered with words right:
"He is not here, for whom ye wend;
He is risen as he you kenned,
And unto Galilee forth is passed."
Then cheer and comfort 'gan amend,
For Resurexit! Non mortuus est!


To tell this tale I hied me fast,
That Filius Regis was risen again;
By a temple, as I forth passed,
I heard a weeping with much pain:
A woman I saw there at the last,
That I first met, I do not feign,
Full doleful on me her eyes she cast,
And how she fared to ask I was fain.
"Alas!" she said, "I am not fain
To see my son in his decease."
Then to that lady I answered again,
Said "Filius Regis non mortuus est!"


Saint Thomas says, and other doctors a heap,
That first he appeared to our Lady dear:
His death to her heart sank most deep,
For she was most unto his cheer.
So bright, so glorious came the Son,
His shining marks his body bare,
He saluted his Mother with great worship;
The words of that saluting are
"Salve sancta parens" I trow they were—
In Latin 'tis written full honest—
"My blessèd Mother for evermore!"
For Resurexit! Non mortuus est!

This was great marvel for to see
The earthly mother that King sustain.
Such joy and such solemnity
Before nor after were never seen.
The earth is glad, the sun is free,
The sun is glad it shall brightly beam,
Nor ever after so black be seen;
The world is glad that grace hath seen;
All Christian people glad shall be,
That Christ is now both King and Priest:
Now is said, hic dies, for joy, I ween,
That Resurexit! Non mortuus est!

Harl. MS., *c.* 1420
Lambeth MS., *c.* 1430

## "SINCE I FOR LOVE"

SINCE I for love, man, bought thee dear,—
Thyself the sight thou mayst see here;
I pray thee heartily, of good cheer,
          Love me again:
That give to me for thee tholed all this pain.


If thou thy life in sins hast lead,
Mercy to ask be not a-dread;
The least drop I for thee bled
          May change thee, son;
All the sin this world within though thou hadst done.


I was wrath righter at Judas
For no mercy would he ask,
Than was I for the great trespass
          That he Me sold—
I was ready to give mercy, ask if he would!


Cain when he his brother slew
Might have had mercy well and true,
But wanhope him from mercy drew,—
          He would ask none:
For this to hell therein to dwell his soul is gone.

Paul, Magdalene and other more,
That in this life wrought mickle sore,
But mercy never passed them o'er
                    When they did ask:
Their asking in all things, they held it fast.


Me think full loath, for sooth, to tine
That I have bought with mickle pine:
The default it will be thine
                    If I thee mourn:
Ask mercy, thy father I and thou my bairn.


Lo where I hold up my hands displayed,
As to receive thee ready made;
That I great love once to thee had
                    Thou mayst well see:
Some love again I am full fain thou wouldst give me.


Instead of love I ask nought of thee
But fainness from thy sins to flee,
And to live aye in honesty
                    Both night and day:
Then my bliss thou shalt not miss that lasteth aye!

Makculloch MS., 15th cent.

# PATER AND CREDO

## I

ALMIGHTY God, our Father of heaven above,
Blessed be Thy name, with us hallowèd alway:
Come might Thy kingdom to all that can Thee love;
Done be Thy will on earth, as is in heaven aye;
Our daily bread Thou give to us this day;
Forgive our debts, as we our debting men:
Let no temptation mar us that we suffer may,
But from all evil deliver us. Amen.

## II

I trow in God, the Father Almighty,
Maker of heaven and earth, and everything,
And in His Son, Christ Jesu, verily,
I trow, our only Lord and heaven's King:
Who was conceivèd-of by the working
Of the Holy Ghost, and born without a sin
Of Mary mild, and she a clean virgin:
Under Pontius Pilate tholèd He to be
Crucified dead, and earthed in His body,
His soul to hell down-passed, then after He
The third day rose from death, and bodily
Ascended into heaven, where now He sitteth by

His Father's own right hand; and from thence in His
    stead
He is to come to judge both quick and dead.
I trow unto the Holy Ghost and firmly
In holy kirk and in the sacraments all,
Where through to have forgiveness holily,
If we repent our sinnings great and small:
Since after that on Doomsday we shall all
In flesh and bone, in body and soul again
Rise and a life aye-lasting live. Amen.

Makculloch MS., 15th cent.

## MIRABILE DICTU

HEARKEN to my tale that I shall show to you,
For of such marvels have ye heard but a few;
If any of them be lies I tell you hereinafter,
I would I were as poor as the Bishop of Chester!
As I rode from Dover to Durham I found by the street
A fox and a polecat had fifteen feet;
The scate stalked o'er the hill and turncoated her skin;
At the kirk-door called the codling and bade let him in.
The salmon sang the high mass, the herring was the
    clerk,
On the organ played the porpoise, that was a merry
    work!
There was a goodly offering in the kirk that day,
For there was all I reckon up in this good array:
There were weasels and wasps offering cart-saddles,
And potted mosquitoes gave cauldrons and ladles:
The pike and the perch, the minnow and the roach,
The mackerel and the stickleback, the flounder and the
    loach.
The haddock hied him, behind he would not be,
With him rode the stockfish that seemly was to see:
Yet were there more, if I truly tell my tale,
The conger and the weasel rode in on the plough tail.
The turbot and the thornback and the great whale:
The crab and the lobster yet there were they all,

The oyster had two horseshoon and offered them withal,
Each took a penny from his purse and offered at the
    mass:
The oyster offered twopence and said he would pay no
    less.
When they this offering made, the sooth if I shall say,
When Midsummer Even fell, that year, on Palm Sunday.
Furthermore forth I went, and more marvels I found:
A puss-hare by a fire roasting a greyhound.
There were diverse meats, could I tell them with my
    mouth,
Saw I never none such, by north nor by south.
There was roasted bacon, mulled bread, new-soured ale,
Whetstones and firebrands chopped up in kale,
There were cobblers in syrup, saddlers in a stew,
Pounded millars, of such have I seen full few,
Millstones in a mould, and cartwheels hard-baked,
Grindstones in gruel and pestles in a cake;
There were castles in Spain, well peppered in paste,
They were flavoured with charcoal, for there was no
    waste:
There were tinkers in tartlets, the meat was very good.
The sow sat him down on a bench and harped of Robin
    Hood.
The shovel shouted on the schawm, the turbot trum-
    peted to that,
The fox fiddled, the rat riddled, thereto clarioneted the
    cat.
In symphony sang the snipe, the lark bowed to all,
The bumblebee handled the hornpipe, her fingers were
    small.
The goose gargled evermore, her gamut was good to
    hear,
Heard I never such mastery, not this seven year!

Then came in misfits in morses to show,
Mallets and beanstalks for they might not go,
Pot-sticks and pan-lids and great long bats,
Hammers and hornspoons and striped mussled cats.
Mock frocks and dressing-gowns came trotting on a
    sparrow,
The hare came with a long gown driving the harrow;
Rattons and mousekins with long cart whips,
Gnats and snails came in a rout of ships,
Cabbages and corbels in great wheelbarrows,
Twenty-six salt eels, each with a sheaf of arrows.
Two forms and a stool rode on one mass-book,
Fifty firebrands and each with a crook:
Door-hinges stalking on stilts in the hands great oaks
    shook.
The sturgeon stood behind the door, sharpening the
    steaks:
The bear was the good cook that all this mirth makes.
All this I saw, that here have I told,
And many marvels more, upon Cotswold.
The throstle and the popinjay sang with the nightingale.
If all this be true that is here in this tale,
God as He made us, mend us as He may,
Save us and send us some drink for this day!

Advoc. Lib. MS., 15th cent.
MS. (temp. Edward IV)

# THE QUEST OF SAINT TRUTH

A MAN that would of Truth tell
With great lords he may not dwell;
In true story, as clerks tell,
  Truth is put in low degree.

In ladies' chambers he cometh not,
There dare Truth not set his foot:
Though he would, yet he may not,
  Come in among their company.

With men of law he hath no space,
They love truth in no place;
Methinks they have a sorry grace
  That truth is put at such degree.

In holy church he may not sit,
From man to man they will make him flit,
It rueth me sore, in mine own wit,
  Of Truth I have a great pity.

The religious who should be good—
If Truth come there, I hold him mad:
They will rend from him coat and hood,
  And make him bare from them to flee.

A man that would of Truth espy
He must seek especially
In the bosom of Mary:
  For there in sooth
  Is Truth.
God be with Truth where he may be,
I would he were in this country!

Sloane MS. (temp. Henry VI)

## "NOW WOULD I FAIN"

NOW would I fain some mirth make,
  All only for my lady's sake
      And it would be:
But I am now so far from her,
      It will not be!


Though I be long out of your sight,
I am your man both day and night
      And so will be.
Wherefore would God as I love her,
      That she loved me!


When she is merry, then am I glad,
When she is sorry, then am I sad;
      And cause why?
For he liveth not that loveth her
      As well as I.


She saith that she has seen it written,
That seldom seen is soon forgotten;
      It is not so:
For, in good faith, save only her,
      I love none so.

Wherefor I pray both night and day,
That she may cast care away
        And live in rest;
And evermore wheresoever she be
        To love her best:


And I to her for to be true,
And never change her for none new,
        Unto mine end:
And that I may in her service
        For ever amend.

        A. Godwhen (temp. Henry VI)

# CONTINUANCE

CONTINUANCE
Of Remembrance
Without ending,
Doth me penance
And great grievance
For your parting.


So deep you be
Graven, pardé,
Within my heart:
That before me
Ever I you see
In thought apart.


Though I make no complain
Against my woeful pain
But bear it still.
It were in vain
To say again
Fortune's will!

A. Godwhen (temp. Henry VI)

## "WHO CANNOT WEEP COME LEARN OF ME"

SUDDENLY afraid, half waking, half sleeping,
And greatly dismayed, a woman sat weeping,
With favour in her face far passing my reason;
And of her sore weeping this was the reason:
Her son in her lap laid, she said, slain by treason.
If weeping might ripe be, it seemed then the season.
  Jesus, so she sobbed,
  So her son was beaten
  And of his life robbed:
Saying these words, as I say to thee,
"Who cannot weep come learn of me."


I said I could not weep, I was so hard-hearted;
She answered me shortly with words that smarted:
"Lo, nature shall move thee: thou must be converted.
Thine own father this night is dead," thus she retorted.
  "Jesus so my son is beaten
  And of his life robbed."
  Forsooth then I sobbed;
Verifying these words, saying to thee,
"Who cannot weep come learn of me."

"Now break, heart, I pray thee! This corse lieth so
    ruely,
So beaten, so wounded, and treated so foully!
What wight may behold and weep not? No one truly,
To see my dear dead Son bleeding so newly!"
        Ever still she sobbed,
        So her son was beaten
        And of his life robbed;
Renewing these words I say to thee,
"Who cannot weep come learn of me."


On me she cast her eyes, and said, "See, man, thy
    Brother."
She kissed him and said, "Sweet, am I not thy Mother?"
And swooning she fell: 'twere hard to discover,
I wit not the more deadly, the one or the other.
        Yet she revived and sobbed
        How her son was beaten
        And of his life robbed.
"Who cannot weep," this is the lay:
And with that wording she vanished away.

Trin. Coll. MS., 15th cent.

# ALL'S WELL!

NOW is weal and all things aright,
  And Christ is come as a true knight;
For our Brother is king of might
The fiend to drive and all of his;
Thus the fiend is put to flight,
And all his boast abatèd is.


So then 'tis good that we should do:
For there is none but one of two:
Heaven to get or else forgo,
Other way none other is.
I counsel ye, since it is so,
That ye will work to win you bliss.


Now is well and all is weal,
And right well, so have I bliss;
And since all things are so well,
I rede we do no more amiss.

15th cent.

# "AMEND ME AND PUNISH ME NOT"

HOLY Writ saith no thing soother,
That no man should pain another;
Since that I am in God thy brother,
            Amend me and pain me not.

This in the Gospel each man may see:
If thy brother trespass on thee,
Between ye two corrected he be;
            Amend me and pain me not.

If thou seest greatly I do amiss,
And no man wot but thou of this,
Make it not out as ill as it is,
            Amend me and pain me not!

Punish no man with thy word,
Neither in earnest, nor jest at board;
Guard thy tongue that is thy sword:
            Amend me and pain me not.

Look that thou no man defame,
Nor punish any's fame;
Right as thou wouldst have the same:
            Amend me and punish me not.

Now to amend, God, give us grace
Of repentance and very space,
And in Heaven to see His face,
            Where all amends and paineth nought.
                                    15th cent.

## "ET INCARNATUS"

MAN, be joyful and mirth make,
For Christ is made man for thy sake!

Man, be merry, I thee rede,
But beware what mirths ye make;
Christ is clothèd in thy weed,
And He is made man for thy sake.

He came from off His Father's seat
Into this world, to be thy mate;
Man, beware how Him thou treat,
For He is made man for thy sake.

Look thou mercy ever cry,
Now and alway, early and late;
And He will set thee wondrous high,
For He is made man for thy sake.

15th cent.

# THE JOLLY SHEPHERD WAT

C AN I not but sing "hoy"
When the jolly shepherd made so much joy.


The shepherd upon a hill he sat,
He had on him his tabard and hat;
His tarbox, his pipe and his flagon he's got,
His name was callèd jolly, jolly Wat:
For he was a good herd's boy.
                              But hoy!
For on his pipe he made so much joy.
I cannot but sing hoy!
When the jolly shepherd made so much joy!


The shepherd was laid upon a hillside,
His dog was to his girdle tied;
He had not slept but a little tide
But "Gloria in excelsis" was to him cried.
                              But hoy!
The shepherd on a hill he stood,
Around about his sheep they stood;
He put his hand up under his hood,
He saw a star as red as blood.
                              But hoy!

"Now farewell Mall and also Will,
For my love go you still,
You I come again until;
And evermore well ring thy bell, Will!"
                              But hoy!
"Now must I go where Christ is born;
Farewell, I come again the morn.
Dog, keep my sheep well from the corn
And warn well Warroke when I blow my horn."
                              But hoy!
When Wat to Bethlehem come was
He sweat: he had gone faster than a pace;
He found Jesu in a simple place
Between an ox and an ass.
                              But hoy!
The shepherd said anon out-right:
"I will go see yon fairest sight,
Where the angels sing in the height
And that star that shineth so bright."
                              But hoy!
"Jesu! I offer thee here my pipe,
My coat, my tarbox and my scrip;
Home to my fellows now will I skip,
And also look unto my sheep."
                              But hoy!
"Now farewell mine own herdsman Wat."
"Yes, for God, Lady, my name is that:
Lull well Jesus in thy lap,
And farewell, Joseph, with thy round cap."
                              But hoy!
"Now may I well both hope and sing
For I have been at Christ's bearing.
Home to my fellows now will I fling,

144

Christ of heaven to his bliss us bring."
                              But hoy!
For in his pipe he made so much joy!
Can I not but sing hoy,
When that jolly shepherd made so much joy.

Hill MS., c. 1518

## "UPON A LADY FAIR AND BRIGHT"

UPON a lady fair and bright
   So heartily have I set my thought,
In every place, wherever I light,
On her I think and say right naught.   Noel!

She bare Jesu full of pity,
That all this world with his hand hath wrought,
Sovereign in mind she is with me,
For on her I think and say right naught.   Noel!

True love, look thou do by me right,
And send me grace, that to bliss I be brought:
Mary, Mother most of might,
On thee I think and say right naught.   Noel!

God that died upon the rood,
Grant that all men to bliss be brought;
Unto Mary I made my mood,
For on her I think and say right naught.   Noel!

Hill MS., c. 1518

## MUTIS MUTANDIS

WOULD God that men would see
   Heartily how things be,
For things that are untrue.
If it be as I ween,
The thing that seemeth green
Is oft faded of hue.

Self-will is ta'en for reason,
True love for fancy chooseth
And no man thinketh shame;
Trust is full of treason,
Each other men accuseth,
No man himself will blame.

This world is variable,
Nothing therein is stable,
Assay howso we will.
Since 'tis so mutable,
How should men here be stable?
They may not, by no will.

When broom will apples bear
And hemlocks honey wear,
Then seek rest in this ground.

With no man is there peace,
No rest nor heart's release;
And few are sure and sound.

Since then there is no rest,
I hold it for the best,
God for our friend;
He that is our Lord
Deliver us with his word,
And grant us a good end.

15th cent.

# A BALLAD AGAINST LONG-LOVING

UP sun and merry weather,
Summer draweth near!


Sometime I loved, so do I yet,
In steadfast wise and not to flit:
But in danger my love was knit,
       A piteous thing to hear.


For when I offered my service,
I to obey in humble wise,
As fervent as I could devise
       In countenance and cheer,


Great pain for naught I did endure,
And all for that wickèd creature.
He and no more, I you assure,
       Overthrew all my matter!


But now, I thank his gift of hand,
I am escaped out of his band,
And free to pass by sea or land
       And sure, from year to year.

Now may I eat and drink and play,
Walk up and down from day to day,
And harken what these lovers say,
      And laugh me at their manner.

When I shall sleep I have good rest,
Sometime I had not all the best:
But ere I came unto this feast,
      I bought it all too dear.

All that affray is clean gone o'er,
Not only that but many more:
And since I have escaped so,
      I think to hold me here.

But all that crew that suffer smart,
I would they had an equal part,
That they might sing with merry heart
      This song withouten fear:

Up sun and merry weather,
Summer draweth near!
      Bib. Pub. Camb. MS., 16th cent.

SING we to the Trinity,
Parce mihi, Domini!

Game and earnest ever among,
And among all other degree,
It is good to think on the Son,
       With parce mihi, Domini.

When thou risest from thy rest,
Make a cross upon thy breast;
I make this song for no vanity,
       With parce mihi, Domini.

Go thou to church and hear thy mass,
And serve God with humility;
Ask forgiveness of thy trespass,
       With parce mihi, Domini.

When thou comest home to thy table
Thou art served with great dignity;
Hold this song for no fable,
       With parce mihi, Domini.

Pray we both night and day
The great God in Trinity,
That hence God teach us the way,
       With parce mihi, Domini.

              15th cent.

# A LAMENTATION OF THE VIRGIN

OF all women that ever were born,
That bear children, abide and see
How my son lieth me before,
Upon my knee, ta'en from a tree.
Your children you dance upon your knee
With laughing, kissing and merry cheer;
Behold my child, behold now me,
For now lies dead my dear son dear.

O woman, woman, well is with thee!
Thy child's cap thou puttest on,
Thou combest his hair, his colour see;
Thou knowest not well how to be done.
But ever, alas! I make my moan
To see my son's head as it is here;
I pick the thorns out, one by one,
For now lies dead my dear son dear.

O woman, a chaplet thou chosen hast
Thy child for to wear to thy great liking:
Thou fast'nest it on with great solace,
And I sit with my son, sorely weeping!
His chaplet is thorns sorely pricking,
His mouth I kiss with sorrowful cheer;
I sit weeping and thou singing,
For now lies dead my dear son dear.

O woman, thou takest thy child by the hand
And say, "Sweet son, give me a stroke";
Sorely bleeding are my son's hands,
No joy have I on him to look.
His hands he suffered for thy sake
Thus to be bored with nails and spear;
While thou makest mirth, great sorrow I make,
For now lies dead my dear son dear.

Therefore, women, by town and street,
Your children's hands when ye behold,
Their breast, their body and their feet,
Good were to think on my son and ye would;
For care has made my heart full cold,
To see my son with nails and spear,
With scourges and thorns manifold,
Wounded and dead, my dear son dear!

Thou hast thy son full whole and sound,
And mine is dead upon my knee;
Thy child is loose, and mine is bound,
Thy child is in life and mine dead is he.
Why was this aught except for thee?
For my child did never trespass here.
Methinks ye are 'holden to weep with me,
For now lies dead my dear son dear.

Weep with me, both man and wife,
My child is yours and loves your weal;
If your child had lost his life,
Ye would weep at every meal:
But for my son weep ye never a deal.
If ye love yours, mine has no peer!
He sends you both goodhap, goodheal:
And for you died, my dear son dear.

Now all women that have your wit,
And see my child on my knees dead,
Weep not for yours, but weep for it,
And ye shall win full mickle meed.
He would again for your love bleed,
Rather than that you damnèd were,
I pray you all to him take heed:
For now lies dead my dear son dear.

To love my son an you be fain
I will love yours with heart sincere.
And he shall bring children and you, certain,
To bliss where is my dear son dear.
                    (*Two verses omitted.*)

                         Rawlinson MS., 15th cent.

# MY TWELVE OXEN

I HAVE twelve oxen that are fair and brown,
And they go a-grazing down by the town,
With hay, with ho, with hay!
Sawest not thou mine oxen, thou little pretty boy?

I have twelve oxen and they be fair and bright,
And they go a-grazing down by the dyke,
With hay, with ho, with hay!
Sawest not thou mine oxen, thou little pretty boy?

I have twelve oxen and they be fair and black,
And they go a-grazing down by the lake,
With hay, with ho, with hay!
Sawest not thou mine oxen, thou little pretty boy?

I have twelve oxen and they be fair and red,
And they go a-grazing down by the meed,
With hay, with ho, with hay!
Sawest not thou mine oxen, thou little pretty boy?

Hill MS., c. 1518

## "PUT MONEY IN THY PURSE"

MAN upon mould, whatsoever thou be,
I warn utterly, thou gettest no degree,
Nay no worship will abide with thee,
    But thou have thy money ready.

If thou be a yeoman, a gentleman would be,
Into some lord's house then put thou thee;
Look thou go spending at large and plenteously,
    And always have thy money ready.

If thou be a gentleman and would be a squire,
Ride about the country as wild as any fire;
I warn thee, friend, thou wilt fail of thy desire,
    But thou have thy money ready.

If thou be a squire and would be a knight,
And darest not in arms to put thee to the fight,
Then to the King's Court hie thee, alight,
    And look thou have thy money ready.

If thou be a lettered man to bear state in school,
A pallium or a tabard to wear hot or cool,
That to busy thyself about, I hold thee but a fool,
    But thou have thy money ready.

If thou be a young man, in list thy life to lace,
About church and market the bishop's will to chase,
What thou mayst get, thou gettest without grace,
        But thou have thy money ready.


If thou havest ought to do, with the Law to plead,
At London, in Paul's churchyard, many for thee will
    read:
I warn thee, come not there! Thy purse will bleed,
        And thou must have thy money ready!
                15th cent.

# LONDON LICKPENNY

TO London once my steps I bent,
   Where truth in nowise should be faint,
To Westminster ward forthwith I went.
To a man of law to make complaint:
I said: "For Mary's love, that holy saint,
Pity the poor that would proceed"—
But for lack of money I could not speed.


And as I thrust the press among,
By froward chance my hood was gone:
Yet for all that I stayed not long
Till to the King's Bench I was come;
Before the Judge I kneeled anon
And prayed him for God's love take heed:
But for lack of money I might not speed.


Beneath of clerks sat a great rout,
Which fast did write with one assent;
There stood up one and cried about:
"Richard, Robert and John of Kent!"
I wist not well what this man meant,
He cried so thickly there indeed:
But for lack of money *I* might not speed.

To the Common Pleas I elbowed through,
Where sat one with a silken hood.
I did him reverence, for so I must do,
And told my case as well as I could,
How my goods were defrauded me by falsehood:
I got not a mum of his mouth for my meed,
And for lack of money I might not speed.


Unto the Rolls I got me from thence
Before the clerks of Chancery;
Where many I found earning pence,
But none at all regarded me.
I gave them my plaint upon my knee,
They liked it well when they did it read.
But lacking money I could not speed.


In Westminster Hall I found out one
Who went in a silk gown of ray,
I crouched and knelt before him anon,
For Mary's Love for help did I pray:
"I wot not what thou mean'st," he 'gan say,
To get me thence he did me rede.
For lack of money I could not speed.


Within this hall neither rich nor yet poor
Would do for me aught although I should die:
Which seeing, I got me out of the door;
Where Flemings began on me for to cry:
"Master, what will ye price or buy,
Fine felt hats or spectacles to read?
Lay down your silver and here you may speed!"

Then to Westminster Gate I presently went,
When the sun was at the height of prime,
Cooks, to me they took good intent,
And proffered me bread with ale and wine;
Ribs of beef both fat and full fine,
A fair cloth they 'gan for me to spread,
But wanting money I might not be sped.

Then into London I did me hie
Of all the land it beareth the prize.
"Hot peascods," one began to cry,
"Strawberries ripe and branched cherries' size."
One bade me come near and buy some spice,
Pepper and saffron they pressed on my heed,
But for lack of money I might not speed.

Then unto the Cheape I had me drawn
Where much people I saw forth stand:
One offered me velvet, silk and lawn,
Another he taketh me by the hand:—
"Here is Paris thread the finest in the land."
I never was used to such things indeed,
And wanting money I might not speed.

Then went I forth by London stone
And down the length of Cannon Street:
Drapers much cloth me offered anon,
Then comes one cried, "Hot sheep's feet!"
One cried, "Mackerel! Green branches!" Another did
     greet,
Bade me buy a hood to cover my head:
But for want of money I might not be sped.

Then I hied me into Eastcheap:
One cries, "Ribs of beef and many a pie!"
Pewter pots they clattered in a heap;
There was harp and pipe and minstrelsy.
"Yea by cock! Nay by cock!" some began cry,
Some sang Jenkin and Julian for their meed:
But for lack of money I might not speed.


Then into Cornhill anon I strode
Where was much stolen gear among,
I saw where hung mine own good hood
That I had lost among the throng.
I knew it as well as I did my creed!
But for lack of money I could not speed.


The taverner took me by the sleeve:
"Sir," says he, "will you our wine assay?"
I answered, "That cannot much me grieve:
A penny can do no more than it may."
I drank a pint and for it did pay.
Yet soon a-hungered from thence I was led,
And wanting money I could not be sped.


Then hied I into Billingsgate
And one cried, "Ho, go we hence!"
I prayed a bargeman for God's sake
That he would spare me my expense.
"Thou scap'st not here," quo' he, "under eleven pence,
I list not yet bestow any alms deed."
Thus lacking money I could not speed.

Then I conveyed me into Kent;
For with the law I would meddle no more:
Because no man to me took intent
I dight me to do as I did before.
Now Jesus once that Bethlehem bore
Save London and send true lawyers their meed:
For whoso wants money with them shall not speed!

Harl., 16th cent.

## "SO RUNS THE WORLD AWAY"

VICES be wild and virtues lame,
  And vice is turned unto a game,
Therefore correction is to blame
That lessens so his dignity.
              God, that sitteth in Trinity,
              Amend this world, if Thy will be!

Patience hath taken hence a flight
And melody is out of sight;
Now every lad must seem a knight,
Report himself as good as he.

In the head of every state,
In courts men make a great debate,
While peace standeth without the gate
And mourneth after charity.

Envy is thick and love is thin,
The most amongst our Christian kin,
For love is without and envy within,
And so kindness away did flee.

Fortune is a marvellous chance,
And envy causeth great distance
Both in England and in France;
Exiled is benignity.

Now let us pray, both one and all,
And specially upon God call,
To send love and grace among us all,
Among all in Christianity.
God, that sitteth in Trinity,
Amend this world, if Thy will be!

Hill MS., *c.* 1518

## "FAREWELL, THIS WORLD"

FAREWELL, this world! I take my leave for ever,
I am arrested to appear before God's face.
O merciful God! Thou knowest I would liefer,
Than all this world's goods, have an hour's space
To make amends for my great trespasses.
Mine heart, alas, is broken for that sorrow;
So am I for this day, that shall not be to-morrow.


This world, I see, is but a cherry-fair;
All things pass; and so is all my gait.
This day I sat full royally in a chair;
Till subtle death came knocking at my gate,
And unavised, he said to me, "Check-mate."
Lo, how suddenly he maketh a divorce!
And worms to feed, here he hath laid my corse.


Speak soft, ye folks, for I am laid asleep,
I have my dream; in trust there is much treason.
Out of death's hold I fain would make a leap;
But all my wisdom is turned to feeble reason.
I see this world's joy lasteth but a season!

This feeble world, so false and so unstable,
Promotes his lovers but a little while;
He giveth them at last but a fool's bauble,
When his painted troth is turned even to guile.
Experience causeth me this sooth so to compile,
Thinking this, over late, alas, that I began:
Folly and hope deceiveth every man.


Farewell, my friends! The tide abideth no man;
I must depart hence, yea, and so shall ye.
But, in this passage, the best song that I can
Is "Requiem Aeternum"; I pray God grant it me,
When I so end all mine adversity,
Grant me in Paradise to have a mansion
That shed His very blood for my redemption!

Hill MS., c. 1518

## "THERE IS A FLOWER"

THERE is a flower sprung of a tree,
    The root of it is called Jesse,
A flower of price;
There is none such in Paradise.

The flower is fresh and fair in hue,
It fadeth never, but ever is new;
The blessèd stock whereon it grew
It was Mary that bare Jesu;
A flower of grace;
Of all flowers solace and pride of place!

The seed thereof from God was bound,
God himself sowed it with his hand,
In Nazareth, that holy land,
And a maiden it found.
A blessed flower;
It springeth never but in Mary's bower.

Gabriel greeted that maid on his knees set,
The Holy Ghost with her he met;
Between them two that flower was set
And kept it is, as due for debt,
And of king's clan.
In Bethlehem to sprout it began.

When that flower began to spread,
Blossom and to come to seed,
Rich and poor in very deed
Wondered how that rose might breed;
Till on a day
Herdsmen came that flower to assay.

Angels came out of their tower
To look upon that fairest flower;
Whole it was in his colour,
And whole it was in their ardour
To behold
How such a flower might spring from mould.

Of lily white and springing rose,
Of fleur-de-lys and primerose,
Of all flowers do I devise
The flower of Jesse beareth the prize,
For most of all
To help our souls both great and small.

I praise the flower of good Jesse,
O'er all flowers that ever shall be
Uphold the flower of good Jesse
And worship it for full beauty,
For best of all
That ever was or ever be shall!

There is a flower sprung of a tree,
The root of it is called Jesse;
A flower of price,
There grows none such in Paradise.

Hill MS., *c.* 1518

# THE BALLAD OF KIND KITTOK

MY grandam was a gay wife, but a fair-made
friend;
She dwelt far away in France, on Falkland fell:
They called her Kind Kittok, so well was she kenned,
She was very like a cauldron-crook, clear in the chimney
well.
They gossip she died of thirst and made a good end.
After her death she dreaded nought in Heaven to dwell;
And so up to Heaven the highway fearless she would
wend,
Yet she wandered, and came to an eldritch well;
    And there she met, as I ween,
    A newt a-riding on a snail,
    She cried, "O'erta'en fellow, hail!"
    And rode an inch behind the tail,
    Till it was near even.

So she had hoped to be horsed to her resting;
At an alehouse near Heaven night fell on them sore:
She died of thirst in this world, that made her so thirst-
ing;
She ate never meat, but drank down a measure and more.
She slept on until morning after nones, and rose up
early;
Fast fared she forth to the gate of Heaven's door,

And by Saint Peter, in at the gate, she poked in privily;
God looked and saw her letting-in, and laughed His heart
    sore.
        And there, for years seven,
        She lived a good life,
        And was our Lady's henwife,
        And held Saint Peter in strife,
        Aye while she was in Heaven.

She looked out on a day, and she thought very long,
To see the alehouse beside the way, till an evil hour:
And out of Heaven by the high gate, the wife was gone,
For to get a fresh drink, the whole of Heaven's was
    sour.
She came again to Heaven's gate when the bell rang;
Saint Peter hit her with a club, which a great clout
Raised on her head behind, because the wife said wrong;
Then to the alehouse again she ran, the pitchers to pour
    out:
        There to brew and bake.
        Friend, I pray you heartily,
        Drink with my grandam, when ye gang bye,
        Once, for my sake.

                      William Dunbar

## "JERUSALEM, REJOICE FOR JOY!"

JERUSALEM, rejoice for joy,
Jesus, the star of most beauty,
In thee is risen as righteous Roy,
From darkness to illumine thee!
With glorious sound of angel glee,
Thy Prince is born in Bethlehem,
Who shall thee make of thraldom free:
Illuminare Jerusalem!

With angels' light in legions
Thou art illumined all about;
Three kings of stranger regions
To thee are come with lusty rout,
All dressed with diamonds about,
Reversed with gold in every hem,
Sounding together with a shout:
Illuminare Jerusalem!

The regnant tyrant that in thee reigned,
Herod is exiled and his offspring;
The land of Judah that chose wrong,
And risen now thy righteous King:
He is so mighty, so worth a thing,

When men his glorious name do name,
Heaven, earth and hell make inclining:
Illuminare Jerusalem!

His coming knew each element,
The air by stars did him perceive,
The water when dry he on it went,
The earth that trembled and did cleave;
The sun when he no lighting gave,
The cross when 'twas despisèd then,
The stones when they in pieces clave:
Illuminare Jerusalem!

The dead him knew that rose upright
Whom long time had the earth lain under,
Crooked and blind declared his might,
That healed of them so great a number:
Nature him knew and had great wonder,
Born of a virgin without stain;
Hell when their gates were broken asunder:
Illuminare Jerusalem!

                                   William Dunbar (?)

# ON THE RESURRECTION OF CHRIST

SURREXIT Dominus de sepulchro,
  The Lord is risen from death to life again,
Qui pro nobis pependit in ligno,
Who for our sins upon the cross was slain;
Whom to annoint went Mary Magdalene,
Ibat Maria Salome cum ea;
To whom God's angel thus did answer plain:
Surrexit sicut dixit, alleluia!


That angel's weed was snow-white in its colour,
His face as lightning flaming, strangely bright;
The knights, the keepers of Christ's sepulchre,
Fell down as dead, in terror of his light,
Whom to behold they had nor grace nor might;
Et terra motus est factus in Judea;
The weird of Jesu is fulfilled aright:
Surrexit sicut dixit, alleluia!


Beholding then the brightness of this angel,
The Magdalene and Mary Salome
Abasèd were in spirit, as saith the evangel,
And stood aback. "Be not afeared," said he,
"The Lord is risen, whom ye come to see,

Ipse precedit vos in Galilee;
To his apostles go tell the verity,
Surrexit sicut dixit, alleluia!"


Honour we all the Lord of joy and glory,
Thank all the mighty Champion, the invincible,
That won upon the tree the triumph of his victory,
That broke the hellish dungeon, the most terrible,
And chased the dragon, the hideous and horrible,
Per crucem validissima trophea,
And brought the souls to joy ever permansible:
Surrexit sicut dixit, alleluia!


Praise we the Lord that did in battle bide
For us that had no other help or shield,
Till bloody were his body, back and side,
He was our mighty sanctuary and shield;
When Phoebus' darkness him God's Son revealed
Sanguinea erant ejus cannepea;
He died triumphant, he rose and won the field:
Surrexit sicut dixit, alleluia!

William Dunbar (?)

# MY LITTLE PRETTY ONE

MY little pretty one, my pretty bonny one!
She is a joyous one and gentle as can be;
With a beck she comes anon,
With a wink she will be gone:
No doubt she is a love of all that ever I see.

Of such there are no more, whether she will come or go:
To no man she is foe, that oft can do and say;
With a trick about her so,
To abide or else to go:
As I will, she will, her kind heart will not say nay.

Her hair as bright as gold, her face a thousandfold
More good than can be told, her favour so goodly;
And her eye so lovely cold
That no man but would be bold,
Himself advance to be bold to crave her company.

Now farewell, my pretty one, now farewell, my jolly
one,
Ye are a jocund one and merry as can be!
And my heart is woe to be gone,
To depart far from my bonny one!
No doubt she is a love of all that ever I see!

Brit. Mus. MS. (temp. Henry VIII)

## "WHAT WOULD SHE MORE?"

OF beauty yet she passeth all
Who hath mine heart and ever shall,
To live or die, what so befall—
What would she more? What would she more?

She is so fixèd in mine heart,
For her sake I abide great smart,
Yet cannot from my love depart—
What would she more?

Long have I lived in great distress,
Long have I sought to have redress,
Long hath she been my one mistress—
What would she more?

My one mistress yet shall she be,
As long as life remains in me;
I trust but once she will have pity,
I ask no more, I ask no more.

Oft times to her I have expressed,
I have told her that I love her best,
In hope that I might be redressed—
What can I more?

She saith to me nor yea, nor nay,
But of her power I know she may,
Jess my heart; then can she say,
What would you more?

If she were in such case as I,
That for my sake in pain did lie,
I would her help or else would die—
What would she more?

Seeing that my true heart and mind
Are toward her so true and kind,
Some love in her if I might find—
I ask no more, I ask no more!

      Brit. Mus. MS. (temp. Henry VIII)

## "I SERVE"

I SERVE where I no truth can find,
Wilfully myself I blind,
To sail against the stream and wind;
Where I love best regards me least
And unto me is most unkind.

I hope and all my trust is vain,
I know the cause, and yet, again,
Such foolishness doth in me reign,
I cannot stop, nor yet shift make
To ease my heart from deadly pain.

I can nothing of her attain,
But for my truth, coldest disdain:
One joyful hour, a year in pain,
It is too much. Thus from all such
I purpose surely to refrain.

Brit. Mus. MS. (temp. Henry VIII)

# "I PROMISE YOU"

MY heart is yours now; keep it fast:
Without your favour my joy is past.
I will not change while my life last,
I promise you.

I think me glad and fain to be
Thrall to you where I was free;
I am so bound I cannot flee,
I promise you.

Call me and I come anon,
Refuse me and my joy is gone;
In you I joy, in you I moan,
I promise you.

I joy in that I have your grace,
I moan when pity lacks his place:
Thus resteth all in your sweet face,
I promise you.

You are my wealth, I am your woe;
I think of you wherever I go;
I love you heartily, and no more,
I promise you.

Brit. Mus. MS. (temp. Henry VIII)

# "WELCOME, FORTUNE!"

WELCOME, fortune, welcome again
  The day and hour I may well bless;
Thou hast exilèd all my pain,
Which to my heart great pleasure is.

For I may say, as few men may,
Seeing of all pain I am released,
I have obtained unto my pay
The love of her that I love best.

To me she is so true and kind
That she is worthy to have praise,
For no disdain in her I find:
I pray to God I may her please.

I know none such as she is one,
So true, so kind, so lovingly.
How should I do and she were gone?
Alas, yet, I had liefer die!

When I do hear her name expressed,
For joy my heart doth leap therefor;
I shall for ever love her best,
Until I die: What would she more?

She shall be sure, while that I live,
Until that death doth me home call,
Both heart and body I her give:
If I had more, she should have all.

Brit. Mus. MS. (temp. Henry VIII)

# PROLOGUE TO "THE SATIRE OF THE THREE ESTATES"

THE Father and founder of faith and felicity,
    That your fashion formed in His similitude;
And the Son, our Saviour, shield in necessity,
That bought you in bail and ransomed on the rood,
Redeeming pledged prisoners with His precious blood;
The Holy Ghost, governor and grounder of grace,
Of wisdom and welfare both fountain and flood;
Save you all in this place
And shield you from sin;
And with His spirit you inspire,
Till I have shown my desire:
Silence, Sovereign, I require:
For now I begin.

Sir David Lyndsay

# COLOPHON

SERVE God truly
And the world busily;
Eat thy meat merrily
And ever live in rest!


Thank God highly
Though He visit thee poorly,
He may amend it lengthly
When Him liketh best.

Hill MS., c. 1518

The Westminster Press
411a Harrow Road
London, W.9